Attorney on Call

Attorney on Call

Lessons from a Life in the Law

Bob Whitley

Expert Press

Attorney on Call
Lessons from a Life in the Law

Printed in the United States of America.

Robert E. Whitley
Whitley Law Firm
3301 Benson Drive
Suite 120
Raleigh, NC 27609

1-800-785-5000
www.whitleylawfirm.com

ISBN-13: 978-1-946203-13-7
ISBN-10: 1-946203-13-0

Dedication

I want to dedicate this book to my parents, Jack and Maude Whitley. My dad is mentioned throughout this book, and he taught me so much of what has led to my success, including hard work and honesty. My mom took good hands-on care of me as I grew up, and she was the first one to know that I wanted to be a lawyer when I grew up. She was my biggest fan and was always on my side, whether I deserved it or not.

Contents

Introduction 1

Chapter 1: Rooted in North Carolina 5

Chapter 2: The Early Years 11
- Beginning to Practice 11
- On My Own 14
- Still a Mystery: John's Story 19
- The Porn King of Kinston 22

Chapter 3: How a Lawyer Can Help You 29
- Do I Need a Lawyer? 29
- How to Find a Lawyer 33
- Selecting a Lawyer: Questions to Ask 35
- The Trial from Heaven: Alicia's Story 37

Chapter 4: Driving Lessons 49
- Preventing Accidents 49
- What You Should Know if You Are in an Accident 53
- Documenting Your Case 54
- Dealing with Property Damage 59
- Securing a Rental Car 60
- Evaluating Your Claim 61
- The Trial from Hell: Rose's Story 66

Chapter 5: More Driving Lessons: Bigger and Badder ... 73
- What Makes Trucking Accidents Different 73
- The Sisters Foster 76

Chapter 6: Insurance 101 81
- Know Before You Need To 81
- The Bottom Line on Insurance 85
- The Case for Insurance and Accident Reconstruction: Chase's Story 85

Chapter 7: Resolving Your Case 93
Preparing Your Case 93
Distribution of Funds 103
Subrogation 104
King's Story 105
Chapter 8: When the Worst Happens 109
Wrongful Death Cases 109
Remembering Cody Blue 112
Ashley's Story 117
Chapter 9: Mythbusting 121
Work-related Injuries 121
Do I Need an Attorney for Workers' Comp? 123
Third-Party Claims 125
Social Security Disability 128
Do I Need a Lawyer to Apply for SSD? 130
Chapter 10: Other Personal Injury Cases 133
Premises Liability 133
The Last Mile: Hilda's Story 135
Pharmaceutical Claims 140
Medical Malpractice 142
Nursing Home Negligence 143
Chapter 11: The Whitley Advantage 145
Pumpkin's Story 145
In Conclusion 155
About the Author 159

Introduction

PRACTICING LAW for more than 40 years can teach a person a lot of lessons and it has certainly taught me quite a few. One of the most important lessons I've learned is this: I always need to remember that when an individual or a family has made a decision to hire me as their lawyer, it's important for me to pause, take a moment, and remind myself that this client had many choices for an attorney and chose me. There were probably a lot of people tugging at them to hire this lawyer or that lawyer and likely they were exposed to a lot of TV lawyer ads. I think that it helps the attorney-client relationship—and probably even the outcome of the client's situation—for the lawyer to keep that in mind and do everything possible to make sure that client never regrets that decision. We have got to go full steam ahead for each of our clients to get the best possible results, and also, and just as important, treat them with the respect and attention they deserve. That means we make ourselves available, we return phone calls, and we suffer some right along with them.

We lawyers see a lot of clients, but most people don't see many lawyers. Our first meeting with a new client is probably the first time that client has ever met with a lawyer. It's natural for them to be a little guarded. It's normal for them to be a little nervous and uncomfortable. That's why I think it's important for the lawyer, by whatever means possible, to make the client comfortable, to make the client feel at ease, and to make the client feel free to share any and all information about which you're going to be representing them.

Our firm airs a weekly TV show in North Carolina. Some of the people who call into our show already have attorneys, and they tell me, much more frequently than I would wish, that they're not able to reach their own attorney. They tell me that they've left a number of phone messages, or that they've gone to the office and they haven't been able to see their lawyer in person, for one reason or another. I think it's important, if a lawyer makes a decision to take a case, that he or she also makes a decision to be available to that client, that the client is going to be more than just a case number or a file number. Every client is a human being with a human family who will be affected by whatever is going on in the client's situation. I don't think that I can emphasize this concept too much.

I believe that the public generally has pretty low expectations about how they will be treated by a lawyer, or sometimes, by any professional person. It doesn't take a whole lot to exceed that expectation. I get a sense sometimes, and maybe it's our own profession's fault, that clients expect the lawyer to be a little more aloof, to command the room. But when that happens, the meeting becomes about the lawyer and not about the client. I think that in order to really effectively represent that client, you've got to allow them to let their hair down. And they're not going to let their hair down unless you do that for them first. Be a nice person who just happens to be a lawyer.

There's also a perception that lawyers, as a group of people, will lie, deceive, and say or do whatever it takes to "win." That is simply a false perception. That's not what most lawyers are like and it is not, without a doubt, who I am. I believe in always taking the high road. If we never misrepresent anything, we can set a better example for our profession with our own individual clients. And the truth usually carries the day.

When I used to practice criminal law, the rule for clients was that if you tell me that you committed this crime, I cannot allow you to get on the stand and deny that you did it. I can fight like heck against the evidence and the law, and try to get you off. That's my obligation as your lawyer, but I can't allow you to get on the stand and lie. That's also true in civil cases, which includes personal injury cases.

I think that's a misconception, or misperception, or maybe a myth that some in the public have come to think about lawyers. Somehow personal injury lawyers have gotten a negative public image. I don't know whether it started out with public figures criticizing lawyers, especially trial lawyers, but it's unfortunately become accepted by the general public. I do think we lawyers contribute to it ourselves in some ways. We're not solely responsible, but there are things we do—gaudy advertising, trying to be macho men, acting like we're doing something sneaky to help our clients—that all adds to the misconception.

In this book I will share some stories from my years in the law—true stories about real clients and real cases—that I hope will offer the reader a chance to learn something about the law, but even more importantly, what it takes to be a good lawyer for clients.

A note to the reader: While we have done what we could to protect identities as needed, there may be some readers who will recognize persons or cases described herein. It is certainly not my intention in sharing these stories to cause anyone unnecessary grief, and I apologize if I have unintentionally done so.

Chapter 1: Rooted in North Carolina

I WAS BORN the middle child of five children. I had two older brothers, one younger brother, and the youngest was a girl. I think my mom was going to keep having babies until she had a girl.

My dad was one of the hardest-working people that I've ever known. I didn't realize it at the time because I was a kid growing up in the family, and that's just how things were. He received a scholarship for a year at Wake Forest but had to drop out of school after one year to go back home to work with his family. He grew up in a very poor family during the Depression era. Apparently early in his life he was convinced of the importance of working hard in your life—whatever your job was—whether it was to earn wages, or to support your family, or to support yourself. He must have learned that lesson very well because he carried it over to his five children, particularly the four of us boys.

Because there were five of us, we didn't have as much money as some of our friends, and so I started working small jobs, like mowing lawns, to earn spending money. I remember my dad encouraging me to try to get jobs, even before I was old enough to get a work permit. I started out mowing yards (about 20 a week) and working a paper route, because you didn't have to have a work permit for either of those jobs. I would deliver papers in the afternoons, the local Kinston paper. I did it on a bicycle where I had a big old knapsack-type thing with all the papers. You would fold the papers before you took off on the bike, and then you threw them into the yards and onto the porches.

When I was 14, I remember my dad driving me to my new summer job, working on a tobacco farm. He knew someone at the farm co-op office in Kinston, and he got me a job working in tobacco. In North Carolina at that time you could work shortly after you got out of school in June and you would usually work through about the middle part of July. It was really hard labor, even though I started out at the easiest job, a hander. And over the next three or four summers I became what was called a cropper. I was actually in the field pulling tobacco off of stalks, gathering it in my arms, and then putting it in a truck that was pulled by a mule. One interesting thing I noticed about working in tobacco was that the name of your job described what you would be doing. You were a hander, a cropper, a hanger, or a trucker.

Several years later, I worked with some of my friends on a tobacco farm where there was a harvester. You sat on the harvester that took you down the rows and you could take the leaves off the stalks. That was an easy job compared to cropping on foot as I had done previously.

During the school year, I worked for my uncle. He owned a drugstore that had a soda fountain in it, serving sandwiches, hamburgers, hot dogs, and soft drinks, and I worked there about 20 hours a week.

Along with my various jobs, I also played sports throughout high school: basketball, football, and baseball. I remember playing baseball in the summer, and coming to a game once with the tobacco gum still on my hands. I got behind the plate—I was a catcher—put my gooey hands in the catcher's mitt and pretty much ruined the mitt.

What I brought away from those early work years was the knowledge that I could get along with all different kinds of people. When I was delivering papers, part of the job was collecting from your customers, either by the week or by the month, so I had to knock on their doors or sometimes go into their homes to collect. When I was working in a tobacco field, I was often the only white person in the field or barn, but when I was in school, my classmates were all white. My school didn't become integrated until I was in the ninth grade.

You don't realize it when it's happening to you, but as I look back I realize I had the good fortune of coming into contact with a lot of different people from different social and economic groups, and I liked all of those people. I liked those guys I worked in tobacco with, and I liked my paper route customers, even the ones who didn't pay me regularly. I just liked them all. And they are the very people that I represent now. I don't represent any companies, any businesses, or insurance companies; I just represent individuals.

Along with helping me develop a good work ethic, those early jobs also helped me develop monetary responsibility. When you're spending your own money you just have a tendency to be more prudent than if you were spending someone else's, even your parents'. But I still was not, and am not now, nearly as tight as my dad was.

My dad instilled in me the principles of hard work. And perhaps even more importantly, he taught me to work with integrity and he taught me how to treat people.

I married my high school sweetheart. Mary Page was a year behind me, so when it was time for me to go to college I went to the closest college to Kinston I could find. That was East Carolina University in Greenville, 30 minutes away.

In my freshman year, I was elected president of the freshman class. I was then selected to the Richardson Leadership Foundation, which was a foundation that offered leadership development opportunities for young people. There was an application process that involved essays and an interview; about eight to twelve of us were chosen. We were given opportunities we would not have otherwise had. One time the foundation provided us a trip to New York City that was entirely paid for.

When I ran for vice president of the student government in my sophomore year, the foundation provided some of the money for my campaign. But the most important thing they did was getting us summer jobs. The foundation would pay our salaries during those summer months for whatever work we chose to do and for whatever company would take us. The company didn't have to pay—it was like an internship, subsidized by the foundation. I chose to go to work for Wachovia Bank in Kinston. Then, when the summer was over, I continued to work for Wachovia in its computer center in Greenville. I pretty much worked somewhere all the way through my undergraduate education.

I was elected vice president of the student government, and that was a small paying job. My salary increased when, the next year, I was elected president of the student government. I was also earning some additional money by tutoring high school students in math and doing tax returns for a tax preparer.

As I was finishing college, I applied to graduate school. I had completed my undergraduate degree in accounting, and I was planning to get my MBA at East Carolina. My career goal at that point was to get my MBA and then become a tax lawyer.

When I started looking at law schools, I found that Wake Forest University had a program which you could start in the middle of the year. You could start in January, and by going to summer school, you could finish as if you had started the previous September. That program allowed me to finish law school in two and a half years.

Mary Page and I had married after my freshman year in college, and we were starting our family. At Wake Forest, they had a married student trailer park on campus, and we moved there after my first full year of law school. My son, Whit, was three years old at the time. It was absolutely the best place to live. We had access to all of the track and field facilities and the tennis courts. It was a pretty cool place to raise a kid. And I could just walk to class in the Law School.

I remember one time just being on the Wake Forest campus and thinking, "I can't believe I've really done this. I may even be a lawyer." I felt like I was just this kid from Kinston, North Carolina who wanted to go to law school. Finally being there was just unreal to me.

I kept working, though, just as I had at East Carolina. By the time I started law school I had completed about 20 hours toward my MBA, and that gave me the audacity to apply for a teaching job at a business college in Winston-Salem, where Wake Forest is located. And I got the job! I taught at Winsalm Business College the whole time I was in law school. I started out teaching night classes in accounting and taxes. I was carrying a full-time teaching load, meaning I was in the classroom 15 to 20 hours a week. During tax season I also worked for a tax preparer.

I graduated from law school in 1974. I had finally realized my dream of becoming a lawyer, and it was time to embark on my career. Full steam ahead!

Chapter 2: The Early Years

REMEMBER MY SAYING that I wanted to be a tax lawyer? That's where I started out, but that didn't last very long.

As I was finishing law school at Wake Forest, I was interviewing for jobs, mostly in the eastern part of the state.

I interviewed with a sole practitioner in Jacksonville, North Carolina, who had a real estate and business practice. He wanted someone to handle estates and taxes and I fit that description. Wanting, as always, to keep busy, I did make it clear to him from the beginning that I wanted to dabble in other things like courtroom work. I persuaded him to allow me to get on the criminal indigent list, which is a system whereby people who were declared indigent could have court-appointed lawyers.

Beginning to Practice

Within two months of reporting to work, I had my first jury trial, there in Jacksonville. I represented a married couple who had entered into a contract to purchase a home. For some reason—I don't remember why, maybe they couldn't get their finances in line—but they had to back out of the contract and the realtor would not return their $500 escrow payment. I filed a lawsuit on their behalf for the $500 and it was my very first jury trial.

The realtor was represented by an older attorney. In the courtroom when they called our case for trial, he didn't even have a file. It was obvious that he hadn't done any preparation for this big $500 trial. I, on the other hand, had done a whole lot of preparation since it was my first trial, and we were successful in recovering the $500.

Bob Lock, who was the sole practitioner I worked for in Jacksonville, was in the courtroom to watch the closing argument. Later he told me that as he watched he was thinking of every point I should make. I did eventually make all of those points in my argument, so he was very proud of me. I thought a whole lot of him, so that meant the world to me. But what meant the most was that the jury returned a verdict and returned the $500 to our clients.

Mary Page had not been crazy about us going to Jacksonville. While Jacksonville is only about 45 minutes from our hometown of Kinston, it's also the site of Camp Lejeune Marine Corps Base. So we were familiar with that community, but she was reluctant to go there because it was not Kinston. But in the end, she acquiesced. She got a job teaching in the elementary school, and we bought a little house in Jacksonville. We were going to make it work.

But then a crime spree started. There were two or three incidents of female shoppers at various shopping centers being kidnapped at gunpoint. The kidnapper, wearing a ski mask, would take his hostage into a bank in the shopping center, rob the bank, and then murder the hostage. He would take her back to her car and shoot her. It even happened in a shopping center where Mary Page had been shopping that same day.

That crime spree hit way too close to home for both of us. Mary Page just didn't want to stay in Jacksonville. She put her foot down and said we had to leave. I didn't resist. I was actually scared myself; there was an eerie feeling in the whole community.

So we left Jacksonville after only four months. The serial killer was eventually identified as Marcus Schrader, who worked in the Naval Hospital in Jacksonville. The authorities published photos from the bank security cameras, and one of his coworkers recognized his eyes in the ski mask. He was arrested after we left.

I wasn't sorry to leave Jacksonville, except for leaving Bob Lock. Maybe it was getting my first taste of courtroom work, but it didn't take me long to realize I wasn't going to be satisfied with an office practice. I had handled a couple of criminal defense cases and then I did my trial. I found I was enjoying that part of my practice much more than I was enjoying the tax work.

I learned of a job opening in Winston-Salem, where I had lived during law school, and I took that job, starting in January of'75. It was a tax law firm in the big Wachovia Bank building, which was then the finest building in Winston-Salem. The building was about 30 stories high, and the lobby, where the bank was located, was filled with marble and wood.

So I was going to go to work in that bank building, and I was going to do strictly tax law. Right before I started there, I learned that the reason the firm had an opening for a tax lawyer was that the person who had held the job previously had committed suicide. I should have taken that as a sign.

It was a very structured, commercial law firm, and my only experience of working in a firm had been with Bob

Lock in Jacksonville where the atmosphere was much more casual and unstructured.

The first day I went to work in that firm I realized that I wasn't going to stay. It was when they showed me my office. It was a small office with a desk and just one chair behind the desk. I asked where my clients would sit, and one of the senior partners said, "For the first year or two, you're not going to have any clients that you're going to need to meet." I knew then I wasn't going to stay there.

I started in January and I felt obligated to work through April 15. I remember agonizing about telling them I was leaving. It probably took me at least a month. I went to work every day promising myself that I would tell them that day. I don't know why I dreaded it so much, but once I finally told them, it was easy.

I did work through tax season in April, and then, thinking that I probably wouldn't be able to get another job—my third in twelve months—I decided to open my own law practice. So we moved back to Kinston and I opened my practice: Robert E. Whitley, Attorney at Law.

On My Own

It was May of 1975, and I immediately got on the criminal indigent list so I could take court-appointed criminal cases. I applied to teach at Lenoir Community College and started teaching night school, mainly to veterans who were being paid to go to school after their service. Keeping busy as always, I did everything I could think of as I was trying to establish my practice. I remember doing second mortgage loans for a banker friend of mine. I did collection work—anything and everything.

Shortly after I got back to Kinston, there was a ruling in a federal court case that led to counties like Lenoir being required to provide a child support enforcement division, not only to the recipients of welfare but to anyone who wanted to apply for that service. It was called Title IV–D, a reference to the federal law under which it was established. I immediately applied for that opening with the Lenoir County Department of Social Services and I was hired as the first IV–D lawyer in Lenoir County.

The whole principle of the IV–D program was to collect child support, mainly from dads. Almost all of the families were separated; the dads weren't living with the mother or the child. If a father had custody, we would do the same with the mom. We would force her to pay child support.

The idea was to provide a supplement, or to help pay back the government, for the welfare that the parent was receiving for that child. That often involved, first of all, establishing legal paternity. If paternity was denied and the facts of the case were such that I felt that we could successfully pursue a paternity case, we filed a paternity lawsuit. These were jury trials. I probably tried about 50-60 of these cases. For a young lawyer, that was a wonderful experience because I was getting in front of juries and judges trying cases.

I was proud of what we were doing because we were essentially helping the taxpayers recoup from the responsible parties some of the money that they were paying in welfare.

Every month we had what was called IV–D Court, and a lot of that was holding fathers in contempt for not abiding by court orders. Many of the fathers were unemployed; a lot of them changed jobs regularly. In those days it was much more difficult to get those dads to pay child support than it is now. There's been a lot of improvement in the process. I was with that program for about 15 years and they were beginning to make some progress, to where we could garnish wages if the father were employed and had been delinquent in his child support. I believe that under today's law, the father's wages are automatically garnished whether or not he's missed a payment.

In the paternity cases I was trying we didn't have the DNA testing that we have today. The only thing we had to go on then was blood type—A, B, AB, or O—and all that really did was provide a means to exclude an accused father. For instance, suppose the mother's blood type was O and the child's was A. That meant the father's type had to be A or AB. If the accused father had type B, we knew for sure he wasn't the father. If he did have A or AB blood, all it meant was that he was one of hundreds of thousands of men who could be the father. In my argument to the jury, I would concede that, but then I would point out that unlike all the rest of those thousands of men, he was having sex regularly with the mom.

I learned other little tactics along the way. I would put the baby in the father's lap while he was on the stand, and get him to either agree or disagree that that child looked just like him.

Even when I was practicing, there were new developments in the blood testing. A new technique called HLA white cell blood testing reached about 90-95 percent accuracy. It wasn't like the DNA testing we have today, but it was getting better. So then I could say that the accused father was among only a few thousand men who had the right blood, but again, unlike the rest in that group, he was having sex regularly with the mom.

There was one particular IV–D case that stands out in my mind even after all these years. North Carolina law at that time had a statute of limitations that limited the time period during which you could bring an action to establish paternity of an illegitimate child. Our statute said you had to bring the action within three years of the date of the child's birth or within three years of the date that the putative father last provided support.

The term under the statute referred to children born out of wedlock as illegitimate children—a term which always was offensive to me because I don't think a little baby is the least bit illegitimate—but that was the term for children born to parents who weren't married to each other. If a father had been paying support for a baby, you had three years from the time he last paid support to bring an action. If the father had never paid support, you had three years from the date of the child's birth.

In this case, the dad's name was Ervin Johnson. When we went to court, the daughter was 7 or 8 years old. Ervin, the dad, didn't regularly send money, but from time to time, he had given her money and called it an allowance when he'd see her on the street. We argued that his giving her money within three years of our bringing the action fell within the law.

But during the case I began to think that this might be a case in which we could challenge the constitutionality of that three-year statute of limitations from support or birth. If we abandoned our claim that it was three years from which he had last paid child support, then it would simply be the court having to decide whether or not he was the father. The court concluded that he was the father but—at our request—ruled that the court could not hold him responsible as the father, and could not declare him the father, because of the statute of limitations.

We appealed the decision, and the case of *County of Lenoir vs. Ervin Johnson* was heard in the Court of Appeals on April 15, 1980.

What we did in the appeal was challenge the constitutionality of the three-year statute of limitations. I argued that the statute violated the Constitution's Equal Protection Clause because there was no such statute of limitations in the case of a support action instituted on behalf of a legitimate child. The Court of Appeals agreed and concluded that the statute did unconstitutionally discriminate against illegitimate children in violation of the Equal Protection Clause of the Constitution of the United States.

When that statute was declared unconstitutional, it opened up hundreds of thousands of cases in North Carolina that otherwise could not have been pursued against fathers who failed to pay support.

I was proud of our work on that case and it did not take a genius to know that the old law was wrong. I also gained a lot of experience—learning domestic law, child support, and custody and visitation—and it put me in front of a District Court judge at least once a month, sometimes a lot more than that when we had jury trials. I wouldn't take anything for that experience.

While I was doing that IV–D work, my practice was growing in other ways—criminal law, family law, and the beginnings of my personal injury practice.

I tried my first murder case in 1976. I was two years out of law school. My client, Ronald S., was 18 years old. He was charged with brutally beating and killing a female acquaintance. Before the body was discovered, a police officer ran into Ronald on his way home in the early morning. The officer asked him why he had blood on his clothes. He said he had cut himself and went on home.

Then later, after they discovered the body, the officer remembered that encounter. They took out the high school yearbook, and the officer identified Ronald as the guy that he had run into. The police went to Ronald's home, where they found the blood-spattered clothes he had been wearing. They took the clothes, and they took him down to the station. They questioned him for hours and hours without his parents. He finally confessed.

During the trial he testified that they had just worn him down and that was why he had confessed. I had some technical evidentiary objections.

He received a life sentence. I appealed the evidentiary issues to the North Carolina Supreme Court, but our appeal was denied. And here's how I know I've become an old lawyer: Ronald was convicted in 1976. He served his whole life sentence and he's been out now for about five years. And I am still practicing law.

My most memorable murder case, though, was one that still haunts me in some ways.

Still a Mystery: John's Story

My client's name was John S. He was accused of murdering his wife, Linda. They had been married in Vietnam in the early 1970s.

Linda went missing on July 21, 1981, but the story started earlier than that. Before she disappeared, Linda went to see an attorney about her marriage to John. She wanted to find out if he had been properly divorced from his first wife, Mildred.

John and Mildred had married in 1947 and separated in 1967, but had never technically divorced. Around July 10, John talked to Mildred on the phone and she mentioned having gotten a letter from Linda's lawyer.

On July 21, John picked up his daughter Rosie from school. Mom wasn't home. So John and his daughter went to the grocery store and a few other places. On July 23, two days later, he went to the sheriff's department and reported that Linda was missing.

He also told them that the only thing missing from their house other than his wife was his blue bathrobe.

On September 14, Linda's body was found in a shallow grave located behind a group of pine trees near a cemetery in their small town. The owner of that cemetery later testified that sometime during July, John had asked him if there was a road that went back to behind the cemetery to a row of pine trees. The owner remembered the conversation when he heard about John's missing wife and rumors that there might have been foul play. He went to the area and found the grave.

The cause of death was determined to be mechanical strangulation. A cloth ligature was wrapped tightly around her neck. An expert witness testified that the cloth was made from a blue fabric.

They eventually charged him with her murder. There was testimony from neighbors who'd seen him wearing the blue bathrobe. There was some evidence from her family of John saying, several years back, that the best way to kill somebody was strangulation. There was also testimony from Linda's family that John had acted violently toward his wife in the past.

Nevertheless, it was still a very circumstantial murder case. He denied that he had done anything wrong. His daughter was one of our star witnesses and testified, among other things, that she would hear him crying in his bed late at night after she had gone to bed. She just couldn't believe that he could do anything to harm her mom.

There were no eyewitnesses. There was not really any direct evidence. The closest direct evidence was a blue ligature around her neck that probably was used to strangle her, but all they could say was that it was blue. They couldn't say it belonged to a bathrobe or anything like that.

Other than his asking the cemetery owner about the site, there was nothing to show that John had been in that area or that he had buried her body. There were no shovels discovered. John was in fairly poor health heart-wise; part of my argument was that he wouldn't have been physically able to do it.

I'll never forget meeting with him before the trial and trying to figure out with him what the state's theory would be—their theory of how he killed her and how he took her body to the grave.

There in the jail I said to him, "John, let's just pretend you did do it. Let's talk about where you were. Did you kill her at home? How did you get the body? What's going to be their theory of how you got the body out, buried it, and your daughter never knew anything? Had you done it before Rosie got home that day?" I remember, he went through it all and said, "I kept her in the trunk until Rosie went to bed. Then I took her out. I would have buried her." This was all "let's pretend."

Then I asked him, "What about the glasses?" Linda's glasses had been found about 20 feet from the grave site.

He looked at me. He said, "Bob, I don't know about the glasses. Remember, I didn't do this. I'm just making all this up." For a moment though, I thought, "Man, he is sitting here telling me what he did." He really didn't tell me what he did. He denied it. And to this day, I can't say I could positively vote beyond a reasonable doubt that he did it. I'd have to say no.

The jury did have trouble with it. They were out all day and wanted to stay into the night. My office, at that time, was within 100 feet of the back of the courthouse, and I remember the judge telling me that if they didn't reach a verdict by eight o'clock that night, he was going to declare a mistrial. A mistrial would have been a victory of sorts; you can always do better a second time.

I went back to my office. I remember sitting at my desk watching the clock. I was a nervous wreck. At 10 minutes till eight the phone rang with a call from the courthouse saying the jury was back and I needed to come on over there. They returned a guilty verdict. John was convicted of second-degree murder and sentenced to 35 years.

I still think about that case, though, all these years later. It's still somewhat of a mystery to me whether or not he did it, and if he did do it, how he did it.

That's one case I would love to try again now that I have a few more years under my belt.

The Porn King of Kinston

As my practice grew, into the mid-'80s, I took on a partner who was a corporate lawyer. He happened to represent a lot of retail stores across the state, including some adult video stores.

Around that same time, the North Carolina legislature changed the crime of disseminating obscenity, making it a felony instead of a misdemeanor. This was during the Reagan presidency, when there was a lot of talk in the national media about the evils of pornography.

Sure enough, one of my partner's clients, a video store owner in Wilmington, North Carolina, was the first to be charged under the new law. Since I was the trial lawyer in the firm, my partner, Everett, enlisted me to try the case with him at my side.

Obscenity is legally defined as sexually explicit material that appeals to a prurient interest in sex. The word prurient is important there—I used to have a little flash card that I showed the jury because I told them it took me a long time to be able to say that. It means sick or morbid, so a prurient interest in sex would be a sick or morbid interest in sex that lacks substantial political, cultural, artistic, or scientific value.

There's no uniform national standard; something that's legally obscene in one jurisdiction may not be considered obscene in another. It's what's called the community standard. The basic guideline for the jury is whether the average person, applying contemporary community standards, would find that the work, taken as a whole, appeals to the prurient interest, whether the work depicts or describes in a patently offensive way sexual conduct specifically defined by state law, and whether the work, taken as a whole, lacks serious literary, artistic, political, or scientific value.

That last piece of the definition was how we defended the cases. Of course, the material was sexually explicit. But even if you assumed that it appealed to a prurient interest in sex, it also had to lack any serious literary, artistic, political, or scientific value. I put together a team of experts. One was a professor who taught family counseling at East Carolina University. He was also a marriage counselor with a private practice. I brought in another teacher from Lenoir Community College who had been on the president's committee on obscenity and pornography. We addressed each of the angles: literary, artistic, political, and scientific value.

Our argument was that the material did not lack value. The marriage counselor talked about how he used that material with married couples to help them talk more freely with each other about their sexuality, so that they were able to communicate about it. He felt that it had a significant political value because families and marriages were so important to our country. And then he would say, "And it had an artistic value, because some people really enjoy this."

We had our principles on what we would defend. We had two criteria: first of all, that no one was either actually underage or depicted as being underage in a film. That was taboo and we would not defend that. The second criterion was that no one appeared as being coerced or doing something involuntarily. Everything had to be consensual. That's where I and my experts drew the line on what we thought we could defend.

What we were really defending was the First Amendment of the Constitution. It might sound corny, but that was really a high mark for me. I enjoyed doing that, even if I wish it had been something other than pornography.

In our trials, I would start out by telling the jury, "Look, this is going to be really sexually explicit. Some of you all may feel so strongly about that that you can't listen to the law and be fair, because it's got to be more than sexually explicit for my client to be guilty."

Then I would give examples of how explicit it would be, and I'd just kind of watch them and see. I would ask the prospective jurors a series of questions like, "Ms. Smith, now, you said that you could still be fair, even though it was going to be sexually explicit, but let me be a little more specific with you. You're going to see people having sexual intercourse in this movie. Are you going to be okay with that? Are you still going to be able to be fair after you see that?" What I was trying to do in jury selection was to eliminate anyone who might have some inherent prejudice against these materials.

Of course, during the trial they would play the whole video in the courtroom on a big TV, and it was extremely explicit. What was worse, really, than what was being depicted on the screen was the soundtrack. It was completely uncensored, and they would turn it up really loud.

I remember spending a lot of time figuring out how I would react while the tape was playing, since I would be sitting at that table right in front of the jury the whole time. I felt like some of the jurors would be looking at me. I didn't want to act too interested, or like I was enjoying it, but I also didn't want to act like it disgusted me. It was really kind of a balance, and I had to do it for an hour and a half, or however long the film lasted. It wasn't just a few minutes.

So what I decided to do was sit there and spend the time reading all the U.S. Supreme Court cases on obscenity.

Part of my argument to the juries in those cases was a question: If the government's going to stop us looking at this voluntarily in the privacy of our own homes, what are they going to do next? Somebody can stand on the corner and talk about communism and how great they think it is or talk about Nazism and how great they think that is—and they have the absolute freedom to do that. The way you respond to them is just to counter with your own opinion, if it's different. You don't prohibit them from speaking.

We never lost one of those cases. The closest we had was a hung jury, and the state dismissed it.

That first case was down in Wilmington, which is New Hanover County, and it's a little bit more metropolitan than Kinston. Because it was the very first case under the new law, it got a lot of publicity, including statewide TV coverage. The headline in the Kinston paper read, "Local lawyer successfully defends obscenity charge." In the interview, they asked me how this was going over in town, and I said it was really doing pretty well except for one thing. At the First Baptist Church, where I'm a deacon, I wasn't the most popular person, especially with the preacher.

I guess I thought I could just quietly go and defend these cases outside of Kinston, but I didn't figure on the publicity that first one got. I didn't figure on the aftermath, either. After we won that first case, the rest of Everett's video store clients—and everybody else in that business, whether they were his clients or not—starting sending me material to get my opinion on whether we could defend it in court. So I had all this material stacking up in the trunk of my car. That's when I started calling myself the Porn King of North Carolina—at least around my buddies, with whom I became very popular.

Eventually, they just quit charging people under that law. Still, I feel like I helped contribute to the freedom of speech in North Carolina, even though it was pornography. Different district attorneys who were friends of mine told me that one of the subjects they had at their seminars was how to deal with me defending these cases.

My dad had retired around the time I came back to Kinston and opened my practice. He would go to all of my trials, and he even drove to Wilmington for that first obscenity case. That's the only case he told me, kind of on the sly and in my ear, that he really wasn't crazy about my winning.

During the '80s, the courtroom part of my practice was growing, with the criminal cases, the IV–D cases, and these obscenity cases. It was very clear to me that that's where my passion was.

I was beginning to believe that I was really good at being a trial lawyer. If you're a good baseball player, you get to be on the best team, and you get to bat cleanup, and you get to do all those kinds of things, so I could kind of choose what I was going to specialize in and I loved it.

Things took another turn, though, when a friend of mine started sending me personal injury cases. Bill Hayes was a close friend of mine whom I successfully defended in a DWI case. Bill was an insurance agent in town. He was one of those very outgoing, gregarious, likable characters whose customers or clients would not only buy insurance from him, but would also consult with him about anything that happened to them. Of course, a lot of times they would report being in an accident because you have to report it to your insurance company.

Bill was really happy with the way I had handled his case, and he became a raving fan of mine. I remember getting calls from people who would say, "Bill Hayes told me to call you and he said that if anybody in the world could handle this case it would be you."

These were mostly personal injury cases, and I found that I enjoyed them the most. Usually, these were working people whom I was representing—people like those I'd worked with in the tobacco field, on my paper route, in my neighborhood—the kind of folks I grew up with. That became my passion, and it has been the focus of my practice ever since.

Chapter 3: How a Lawyer Can Help You

AS I SAID in my introduction to this book, my 40-some years of practicing law have taught me a lot of lessons. I've been blessed with the opportunity to work with all kinds of people in all kinds of situations. Along the way I've learned a lot about human nature. As my practice has evolved over the years, I've learned more and more about how best to serve the people who come to me for help. When I meet with a new client, I have the benefit of years of experience and hundreds of previous clients. But for that new client, I'm probably the first lawyer they've ever met.

I believe that part of our obligation as attorneys is to educate people about the law, not only our own clients but the general public as well. So if you're one of those people who might be seeking legal help for the first time, here are some things to consider.

Do I Need a Lawyer?

First of all—and this might surprise you—I do not think that most people who are involved in an accident, and are injured, necessarily need to hire a lawyer.

I do think, though, that anyone who has been injured, even if the injury does not seem serious, should at least get some legal advice. Fortunately for the public, these days there's plenty of information available on lawyers' websites, in lawyers' direct mail advertising, and in general lawyers' marketing. All of these things serve a public purpose in providing information to people who have perhaps have been in some kind of motor vehicle accident. It may be a car accident, or some other kind of vehicle—it could be a truck, a bicycle, a motorcycle, or even a tractor-trailer rig.

There are plenty of good personal injury law firms that will provide free information, and will probably even answer questions without a charge. Our own Whitley Law Firm provides that service free of charge.

I spend a great deal of my time, every day, on the phone with new callers. They've been in an automobile accident, or they have some claim from a wreck, and they just don't feel confident in dealing with the accident's aftermath themselves. They have lots of questions. Sometimes they've done some looking around on the internet but what they've found has only served to confuse them some.

So as an attorney who represents injured people, I think that we owe it to the communities in which we practice to provide as much free information as we can. At the same time, we've got to be willing and able to recommend that someone hire a lawyer, if they really need one.

I will say that everyone who is in an accident and has a claim of any kind, at least needs to consult with a lawyer to get information.

There are some circumstances in which I think you definitely need to retain an attorney. The first is when there is a serious injury. Of course, that begs the question: What's considered a serious injury?

Any injury that results in an extended hospital stay, more than a night or two, should be considered serious. An injury that requires any kind of surgery is serious. Anyone who incurs any type of brain injury, even if it's a seemingly minor brain injury and a concussion, I think needs to hire an attorney. Likewise, anyone who suffers any spinal injury in an accident should retain an attorney.

Now, I'm not suggesting that you hire the first lawyer that you call, but you should at least begin to search for an attorney to hire. Those are all instances in which I think you definitely need an attorney.

Then there are cases that fall into a bit of a gray area. When I'm talking with prospective clients, I sometimes find people who, either because of their age or their level of sophistication, really do need to hire a lawyer. Maybe they don't fit into the category of serious injury, but they at least fall into a category where they just need somebody to help them.

These are people who are not probably going to be capable of dealing with an insurance adjuster and all of the nuances of handling even a not-so-serious claim. I often find that with elderly people or people who can't handle stress. Maybe they have some anxiety issue stemming from the wreck, or whatever reason. That's something I always discuss with callers—whether or not they feel like they can handle it themselves, or whether they have someone close to them, like a spouse, or a child, or a parent, who can help them handle the claim with the insurance company.

You have to remember that dealing with an insurance company about an accident claim is very different from dealing with your friendly neighborhood insurance agent. Many people are familiar with dealing with their insurance agent, who is the friendly person who sells them their policy and who answers questions about their policy. The agent may even become a friend, or at least an acquaintance, of the insured. But when you're dealing with an accident claim, you're not talking to your agent; you're talking to an insurance adjuster.

If you're in a wreck, the insurance company that insures the responsible driver or owner is going to assign an adjuster. An adjuster is completely different from an agent. The adjuster's sole job is to handle claims—to open the file and close the file, pay the claim, and quite frankly, to pay it with as little money as possible.

The adjuster is not like your agent. Agents are usually friendlier, more compassionate people. That's why they don't let agents adjust claims, because sometimes the adjuster is going to deliver some bad news. They may not recognize certain medical expenses that an injured person has incurred, or they may think that their insured driver was not at fault. And in states like North Carolina, which have a contributory negligence law, they may admit that their driver was at fault but try to deny your claim by arguing that you, as the claimant, were also partly at fault. If they can prove that, they won't have to pay anything.

Sometimes I believe that contributory negligence can best be explained by explaining comparative negligence, which is recognized in most states, but not NC. In those comparative negligence states, if the injured party is found to be partly at fault in the wreck, his recovery is reduced by the percentage of his fault. In NC, if the injured party is any at fault, he recovers nothing.

That's why I always think it's important to at least talk with a lawyer before you make a statement to an insurance adjuster. Remember, that adjuster—who wants to talk to you pretty soon—knows all about the relevant law, and knows all the law about contributory negligence. They are trained professionals, and most claimants are not. Even if it's not a case where you need to hire a lawyer, just spending a few minutes on the phone talking about the interview with the adjuster will help you avoid unintentionally creating a defense for the insurance company. A lawyer will be able to help you through that.

There are statistics that say people who use lawyers in their claims generally recover two to three times more than people who do not. I also think that getting a lawyer or hiring a lawyer can give you some peace of mind, particularly when you're dealing with your injury at the same time you're trying to deal with an insurance adjuster.

Having a lawyer on your side will decrease your stress and probably increase your recovery. In fact, I use that as the threshold when I'm deciding to take a case. If I feel that I cannot get the claimant more money in his or her pocket, after my one-third attorney fee, than they could get handling the claim on their own, then it's definitely not a case where they should hire me, and I'll tell them that. The exception would be the peace-of-mind issue, or any stress issue that this particular client is going through.

How to Find a Lawyer

Once you've decided that you need a lawyer, finding one should be no problem. They're on your TV all day long; your mailbox is full of mail and brochures. The key is finding the lawyer who is right for you.

When you're trying to find a lawyer for an automobile accident claim, I always recommend that you find lawyers who do that kind of work. You might already have a family lawyer or estate lawyer, someone that the family knows. You might be inclined to go to him or her with a serious automobile claim, but I think that's clearly a mistake. You want someone who specializes in these cases

Being as old as I am, I will say that the most important thing about selecting a lawyer is the experience of the lawyer. (I think I was saying that 30 years ago, too!) It's not necessarily age as much as it is experience and a successful track record in handling injury cases.

It's important to get a lawyer who has a reputation for fighting with insurance companies when it's needed. You need a lawyer who is willing and able to go to court if that's what it takes. There are wholesale law firms out there who handle a high volume of cases. If you use one of these firms, you typically don't really get to interact with a lawyer very much, if at all. The insurance companies know who these firms are, and they know from day one that they're never going to file a lawsuit in your case. When they know that about your law firm, it diminishes the value of your claim. The only motivation for an insurance company to pay—and the only thing my clients have to negotiate with—is the ability to file a lawsuit and let a jury decide on the value of their settlement.

When I'm working on a case and we've identified the maximum that the insurance company will voluntarily pay, sometimes my clients say, "Mr. Whitley, that's not enough money." At that point, there are only two choices: to accept the insurance company's offer or to file a lawsuit. Here's my point: Insurance companies know which firms never file lawsuits or seldom file them. They also know the ones that might.

At the Whitley Law Firm, we have that reputation, and I think it probably enhances the value of our clients' claims. I'm not saying that our clients automatically receive higher settlements, but I do believe our reputation is an advantage to our clients.

Selecting a Lawyer: Questions to Ask

When you are considering a lawyer to represent you, there are some basic questions you should ask before you hire. The number one question should be: How accessible will the lawyer be? It is absolutely imperative that a lawyer be accessible to the client, throughout the representation. These days, client service and accessibility is often handled by support staff, like case managers or paralegals. I do think that case managers and paralegals certainly provide an important service to a client going through a claim. They gather all the medical bills, the records, and the insurance policies; they identify the adjuster; and they handle paperwork and record-keeping.

But when it gets down to settling a claim, whether it's a very serious injury or not so serious, I believe it's imperative for the claimant to have access to their lawyer and for their lawyer to know them. How else can I be an advocate for clients who are going through a bad time in their lives, as all of our clients are? If I don't know that client, if I haven't had interaction with that client, then I'm not going to know what's going on in their life. I'm not going to be able to get on the phone with the adjuster and say, "Now look, wait a minute. This isn't just the ordinary $20,000 case with $8,000 in medical bills. This person was planning to go to summer school this summer and couldn't do that and had to wait until the fall." Or that they still have this fear of driving because they were involved in a bad wreck. Every case has its nuances, and there is no way for a lawyer—who is your advocate—to understand those nuances unless they've created and sustained an ongoing relationship with you.

Another way to put it, as I mentioned earlier, is that you don't want a law firm that's in the wholesale personal injury business where you never talk to an actual lawyer.

There's one more important question to ask in selecting your lawyer, but this question is for you. How comfortable are you with this person? Why does that matter? It matters because you're going to be sharing very personal information with your lawyer, and you're going to have to share that without reservation. You don't need somebody who is squirrely-eyed, not looking at you when they talk to you, or very seldom talking to you at all.

You need to feel comfortable talking with your lawyer about personal information, and you also need to feel comfortable trusting your lawyer's judgment as your claim progresses. There will come a point when you will have to make a decision—say whether to accept a settlement offer or go to court—and you will have to depend a great deal on your lawyer's opinion. So in order to be able to rely on your lawyer's advice in making that big decision, you want someone who is well-experienced, has tried a number of cases before, and has come to know you well. I always tell my clients that no matter how much they tell me and how thoroughly I read their medical records, nobody knows their injury like they do because they live it every day. But it is my job to be their advocate—to speak for them and to speak loud and clear.

The Trial from Heaven: Alicia's Story

Every lawyer has his or her most memorable cases. I've already shared a couple of mine, and there will be others throughout this book. But this particular case has been dear to my heart for many years. I was still a fairly young lawyer when this case came to me, and it taught me so much about being an advocate for my client in every way.

It was a tragic situation, a wrongful death case. A woman named Shirley Smith came to see me after her 16-year-old daughter, Alicia, was killed in a car wreck.

Alicia Smith had gone to the beach with two other girls. They planned to leave on a Saturday morning and come back at the end of the day Saturday.

Alicia's dad—his name was Hubert, but he went by "Junior"—was reluctant to let her go, but she talked him into it.

They went to the beach and during the course of the day, as teenagers will do, they drank some beer.

This beach is about an hour and a half from Kinston, and there's a back road that's used as a shortcut to this particular beach. These are rural roads and there's a part of the route that's called Snake Road because it's so curvy and winding. So as the girls were on their way home in the late afternoon, the driver apparently lost control of the car on Snake Road. The car flipped over across the low ditch on the road shoulder and ended up in a field next to the roadway, upside down, with the passenger door up.

State troopers came to the scene along with all the first responders. Alicia was dead at the scene. The top part of her body was hanging out the window of the passenger door that was up in the air. Her friend Angela was walking around, frantic and hysterical. The third girl had been passed out asleep in the back seat at the time of the wreck.

Angela told the law enforcement personnel that Alicia was driving and had lost control. The girl in the back seat said that the last time she was awake, Alicia was driving. The state trooper concluded in his report that Alicia had been driving and that she had a crushed chest, which to him was consistent with her having hit the steering wheel before the car flipped.

Alicia's mom, Shirley, showed up in my office with the accident report and told me that she just didn't believe Alicia had been driving. I was cautious; I thought it might have been a denial thing, which is pretty common. I didn't discard her idea, but I was not very hopeful.

I told her I would look into it and I called the officer. I asked him why he had concluded that Alicia was driving. After all, the car was owned by Angela's dad.

He said that the other two girls had told him Alicia was driving, and he didn't think young people like that would be capable of making up something so quickly. He also thought the nature of the injuries was consistent with the girls' account.

Although the first responders had arrived quickly, the first ones on the scene were actually two civilians, neighbors who happened to be riding by. Both of them were quoted as having seen Angela walking around in a hysterical state, saying, "I've killed my best friend. I've killed my best friend."

After I had looked at the accident report, and talked to the witnesses, and talked to the trooper, I gave Shirley my report. There's part of me that always hates to say no—I'm a problem solver by nature and profession—but I couldn't encourage her. I told her that it would be difficult, if not impossible, to prove that Angela was driving. Still, she had so much faith and confidence in me even though I was a young lawyer, and I was her choice to prove that Angela and not Alicia had been driving the car that day.

She came back to me a short time after that. She had Alicia's yearbook in hand, and she was all excited. Alicia had gone to Bethel Academy, a small church-affiliated private school in Kinston. Shirley told me that she and Hubert had been down in Jones County, where Snake Road is and where the wreck had happened. She had heard about some guy who had seen the girls before the wreck, and she had finally tracked him down. He was a country preacher by the name of John Hansley.

Once she located him, on her own, she went to see him, with the yearbook, and, according to Shirley, he identified Alicia's picture in the yearbook as the girl who was in the passenger's seat of the car when the car stopped right next to his pickup truck at the beginning of Snake Road.

Returning home from the beach to Kinston, you make a right turn onto Snake Road. There's a stop sign there. Hansley, in his pickup truck with his grandson, had pulled off on the side of the road just before the stop sign. He was having a discussion with his grandson. As he was parked there, the girls' vehicle passed him, missing their right turn. According to Hansley, the car stopped, backed up and then made the right turn onto Snake Road. When they stopped at the stop sign they were immediately to his left, and he got a good look at the girl in the passenger seat. He identified the girl in the passenger seat as Alicia, based on the yearbook photo.

I told Shirley that we had just barely enough to file a lawsuit, and we filed a wrongful death lawsuit against Angela.

Here's how inexperienced I was: I filed the suit in the wrong court. I filed it in District Court and it should have been in Superior Court. The defense lawyer was Brian Scott, a stately, older man and a distinguished lawyer who had been practicing for many years. He was kind enough to call me and point out my mistake, and consented to my getting the suit moved to the proper court.

So I started out my relationship with this distinguished lawyer by having filed the lawsuit in the wrong court. That wasn't a great start—not exactly a confidence builder for a young lawyer.

Nevertheless, I set about building our case. I was determined to not let Shirley down and to give it my best shot.

In the course of our preparation for the trial, I acquired the car, which had been totaled. It wasn't much, maybe $100, but I wanted to preserve it. I hired a mechanic expert from Greenville, about 30 miles away, because Angela's family was in the auto repair business in Kinston. I wanted to get someone who would not have known the family. The mechanic looked over the car and told me that, contrary to the police report, the steering wheel had not collapsed. The car was a Buick, and like other General Motors vehicles in those days, had a steering wheel designed to collapse with a certain minimum amount of pressure on it. It was intended as a safety feature to minimize the injury to the person hitting the steering wheel. But this one had not collapsed.

Brian Scott, the defense attorney, took Preacher Hansley's deposition and focused on the yearbook identity of Alicia.

We also had to deal with blood alcohol (BAC) results. Angela's BAC came back from the lab as .18, which is more than double the legal limit. The other girl's was about .10 or .15. Alicia's blood alcohol test was lost by the SBI, but I was less concerned about that, since in our theory of the case, Angela had to have been the one driving.

For us to win, we had to prove two things: first, that Angela had been driving, not Alicia, and second, that Alicia was not contributorily negligent. North Carolina law says that it's contributorily negligent to ride with someone that you know is impaired. If you're riding with somebody with whom you've been drinking all day and you get hurt, you're probably not going to have a claim because of your own contributory negligence. If the jury were to find Alicia contributorily negligent, there would be no recovery.

I remember doing a lot of research on that. I did find a case that said sometimes you don't have any choice but to ride with somebody who is impaired. Suppose, for example, that you're out in the country somewhere, and you have no other means of getting home. That was my thinking on that defense. Once she was at the beach, they'd had too much to drink. But how else was she going to get home?

We prepared for trial in every way I could think of. I had a college student, Gene Jenkins, working for me as an assistant. He would later go on to become a law partner (and one of the best lawyers ever in Kinston), but back then he was an undergrad and worked for me in the summer. Gene and I went down to Snake Road in his little sports car. I drove and he sat on the hood with a video camera. We followed that curving, winding route that the girls had taken, right by where

Reverend Hansley had seen them, and we drove to the scene of the accident. I also got an aerial photo of that whole Snake Road. Using the photo and our video as evidence, I planned to argue that there was no way the driver could have driven as far as she did on Snake Road, if she had been impaired.

My theory was that Angela had been the driver, and that she had not been impaired. The blood alcohol test indicated that she was, but that was the only indication. The first responders and everyone who had been on the scene all said she hadn't shown any signs of impairment. I speculated that the lab might have mixed up the blood tests, and that Angela's was the one that had been lost. If the high blood alcohol had been Alicia's, and she had been a passenger, that would not be contributory negligence.

The case finally went to trial, after months of preparation. My inexperience almost tripped me up again in the jury selection.

In a trial, you have eight peremptory challenges that allow you to dismiss a prospective juror for any reason. If you don't like the way they look, you can excuse them, but you're using one of your eight challenges. You also have challenges for cause. If somebody gets up there and says, "You know my daughter was killed in a wreck six months ago and I don't think I could be fair in this case," you can challenge for cause and you don't have to use one of your peremptory challenges. Experienced lawyers have a general rule of thumb that you don't use up all of your challenges because you just don't know who you might get, and you want to keep your options open.

But as I said, I was still a young lawyer and much less experienced than I am now.

I knew the alcohol consumption would be an issue, so I asked every juror their feelings about alcohol. I said there was going to be evidence that all three of these girls had consumed some alcohol, and I asked if they had strong feelings about that, maybe religious or social objections, that would keep them from being completely fair in rendering a decision.

One of the last jurors selected for this panel was an older gentleman (probably much younger than I am now) who had young teenagers of his own. He said, "You know, alcohol is really a big deal in my house." You could see he was thinking hard about it. He finally said, "I will struggle, but I think I could still be fair." If he had said he just didn't think he could be fair in this case, I could have excused him for cause. But he didn't say that. And I had used up all my peremptory challenges. So he was seated on the jury.

The case went to trial. And once the trial finally started, unlike many cases, everything that could go right in that case did. In my mind I still call it my trial from heaven because of how it all unfolded.

Remember the mechanic that we had hired? Over the months between the time we first hired him and the date of the trial, we had never managed to talk to him when he was sober. But he showed up at trial looking like a TV commercial service station attendant, in his clean, white mechanic's outfit. He did an excellent job explaining about the steering wheel not having collapsed. I got Angela to identify it as the steering wheel from her car. When the state trooper was on the stand, I plopped it in his lap so he could show everybody where it was bent, and of course it was not bent. It was perfectly shaped.

Then it came time to put Reverend Hansley on the stand. We had to go pick him up from Jones County. He didn't have transportation. Gene, my assistant, was going to pick him up, and I talked to Gene before he left. It had dawned on me that nobody on either side had ever asked Hansley if he could identify the driver of the girls' car. I told Gene to ask him that. I said, "When you bring him to the courthouse, talk to him about whether or not he can identify the driver." The trial was underway when Gene arrived with Reverend Hansley. I looked to the back of the courtroom and Gene held his thumb up. That was the only signal that I had, but I knew what the answer was.

When I did call Hansley to the stand, we went through the yearbook photos and how he had identified Alicia as the passenger. Then I said, "Now Reverend Hansley, did you have an opportunity to see the driver of the vehicle as clearly as you got to see the passenger?" He said, "Oh, yes."

In fact I believe he said, "I could even see her better. She was closer to me." I said, "Well, could you identify her if you saw her?" And he said, "Yes."

"Well, do you see that same girl who was driving? Is she in the court room today?" I've never seen a witness do what he did. He just turned immediately to his far left, because he was sitting to the right of the jury box and he started looking, almost individually, at each of the jurors. He then looked up at the judge and then he kind of swung around and looked across the court room. When he got to Angela, sitting at the table with Brian Scott and another lawyer from his law firm, he just stopped and said, "That's her. She was driving."

It was one of those Perry Mason moments that usually only happen on TV. Nobody had any clue that this was coming. With discovery, and depositions, and all the normal pretrial preparation, these kinds of surprises just don't happen, but this was literally a Perry Mason moment.

I put Alicia's parents on the stand. Shirley did as good a job as I've ever seen a parent do in a death case. She used the opportunity to share Alicia's life with all of those jurors. We had a big poster with her cheerleading picture on it; we had a picture of her sitting on her daddy's pickup truck with her daddy. Shirley just brought her to life. We didn't have the luxury of video then, or all the stuff we'd have today, but she did it in such a way that she was smiling, and able to laugh at times talking about Alicia, and she was just excellent.

Then Hubert got on the stand and identified himself. When I asked him to tell the jury what he missed most about Alicia, he couldn't talk. He didn't cry, but you could tell he just couldn't talk. Judge Tillery called a recess, and Hubert returned to the stand after the recess, but he still wasn't able to stay a word. So I just excused him.

It was a big contrast to Shirley's testimony, but they were each equally powerful in different ways.

And then it came time for Angela to take the stand. I asked her why she was telling those people at the accident scene that she had killed her best friend if she had not been driving. With a real mean look on her face, she just indifferently said, "Well, she wasn't even my best friend." She was the world's worst witness.

The case lasted five days and Angela's testimony came near the end. The courtroom was getting a little crowded behind me. It had become the Smiths versus Angela's family, with each family and their supporters and others crowding into the courtroom. At one point Angela made this scowling look over my shoulder behind me to one of the spectators. I asked her to turn to the jury and make the same face to them, and believe it or not, she turned and she gave a scowling look to the jury.

That's when the judge—his name was Bradford Tillery; I won't forget him either—said, "Mr. Whitley, you need to go on. That was not a question and you need to ask questions."

In my closing argument, I took issue with the fact that the first responders had treated it like an open-and-shut case. I said, "I really wish the trooper had done a little better job and that we had photographs." Because they assumed it was open-and-shut, they hadn't really taken any pictures of the car or anything. I told the jury, "But you know, I have to speculate to some extent and so will you." There was something in Angela's deposition that I extracted and pounded on. She had said something that suggested she had to crawl over Alicia to get out of the car. So that was what I told the jury. I said, "I think this car flipped. I think Alicia was there on the passenger door with the window down. She crushed her chest as the car flipped over, when it ended up lying on the driver's side." I pointed out that the only evidence of Angela's impairment was the blood tests, and I suggested that the lost test could have been Angela's, not Alicia's. If the high blood alcohol had been Alicia's, she would not have been negligent because she was not driving.

While the jury was out, Brian called me and asked if I would like to talk about a settlement. He offered $50,000 to settle the case, and I presented that to Shirley and Hubert.

Shirley said, "We've gone too far, Bob." Then she reminded me, "Don't you remember the first day I came to you? How hard this was? We've come this far; I'm not going to settle." I pointed out that the jury could decide against us and they would be left with nothing, and more importantly no vindication. But for her, it wasn't the money; it was the principle of the thing. Her daughter was essentially being blamed for her own death. And Shirley wanted vindication for her girl. I learned something from Shirley that day.

During the jury deliberations we got word that the jury had a question from the foreman. They brought the jury back into the courtroom—that's the first time you get to know who the foreman is—and sure enough, the foreman turned out to be that last juror chosen. It was the older gentleman with the teenage kids, and that scared me to death. The jury's request was that they wanted the judge to restate the instruction and law on contributory negligence. I thought, "Oh, crap. This is not good."

Despite that, we said no to the settlement offer. I had recommended to Shirley that she accept it, but she was determined to see it through.

In the end, the jury came back with a $400,000 verdict, which at the time was the largest verdict for a death case in Lenoir County. I heard later that Brian had never had a verdict returned against him for more than $40,000. His partners told me he was in shock.

It was a really powerful moment for the family, in spite of their tragic loss, because they had proven their point that their daughter had not been responsible for her own death.

And as for me, that case stands out as a glowing example of how hard work can prevail, just as my dad had taught me.

That case was long, grueling work—acquiring the car, going down to Jones County, riding that road, videotaping that road, interviewing all the witnesses and the first responders. I was young and inexperienced. I filed in the wrong court. I ran out of juror challenges. I didn't do the smart things but I did the hard work and I did the due diligence things. To me, that's the key to being a good lawyer. It's not necessarily being the smartest lawyer; it's being willing to put the most work into it. And to be just relentless in helping your client prevail.

> *"I was in the courtroom every day of Alicia's trial to support Junior and Shirley. Bob was a young lawyer then, but it was obvious to anyone watching that he was thoroughly prepared and was a relentless advocate for my family. I will never forget the day he walked into the courtroom carrying the steering wheel of the car involved and plopping that steering wheel in the lap of the trooper and asking him to point out where it was bent. It was not bent."*
>
> *~ Betty Jean Jones, Alicia Smith's aunt and sister to Hubert (Junior)*

Chapter 4: Driving Lessons

SINCE I HAVE focused my practice on personal injury law, the most common cases I see are automobile accidents. I've handled many, many accident cases and in this chapter, I'll talk about what to do if you have the misfortune to be involved in an accident.

But having seen so many accidents, I've also learned a few things about how best to prevent them. So let's start there.

Preventing Accidents

In my experience, the most common cause of automobile accidents is distracted driving.

Certainly, the use of a cellphone while driving is a distraction. It's more of a distraction if you're holding it in your hand as opposed to talking hands-free on a Bluetooth device, but it is still a distraction. I've learned from human factors experts that it's not necessarily the physical distraction of looking at the phone or handling the phone; it's the mental distraction of picturing in your mind the person you're talking to or what you're talking about.

One other thing I learned from these human factors experts is that we all do it—that is, we all talk on our phones while driving—and we do it because nothing bad has happened . . . yet.

The distraction isn't always texting or emailing or talking on the phone. It's any kind of distraction that causes you not to pay complete attention to what's ahead of you on the road or to the operation of your vehicle. It's easy to become distracted and not pay attention to how fast you are going and how closely you are following another vehicle.

That's another common cause of accidents: people driving faster than they should and following other vehicles too closely, whether it's in the city where speed limits are much lower or on a freeway where the speed limit may be 60 or 70 miles an hour.

Most drivers underestimate how quickly they can react to a possible collision. Accident re-constructionists and human factors experts say that the average driver has a perception time of about .75 seconds and a reaction time of about .75 seconds. That's a second and a half in total for perception/reaction.

Perception is the time that it takes you to realize that there is some danger ahead of you. Reaction time is the time that it takes you to react to that danger, which when you're driving is putting your foot on the brake. This means that on average, from the time you perceive a situation as dangerous until the time you get your foot on the brake, one and a half seconds have passed. Other factors like your age, the weather, and visibility, or lack thereof, can affect your normal perception/reaction time adversely. Likewise, if you're younger, or if you're actively anticipating danger, your perception/reaction time might be less. The next time you are stopped at a traffic light with other traffic, watch the delay that the first car in line has in moving forward, even though the light changing is clearly anticipated. Nevertheless, there is some perception and reaction time.

Why is this important? When you do the math, the end result is that you are traveling approximately 1.5 feet per second for each mile per hour of speed. For example, if you are driving in city traffic at 20 miles an hour, you're going to go 45 feet in that second and a half before you have your foot on the brake.

That would not always result in a very serious collision, although you can have serious collisions at that speed. Most of the time in municipal areas, you see more fender-benders than you do in rural areas or in freeway driving or interstate driving.

The typical speed limit for North Carolina highways is 55 miles per hour. On some of the interstates, the speed limit is now 70 miles per hour. Now it gets serious. At 70 miles per hour, you would be traveling 105 feet per second. So in your 1.5 seconds of perception/reaction time, you've basically traveled 160 feet—that's nearly half of a football field—before you're even starting to brake. Then, of course, you have a braking distance, since cars don't just stop as soon as you start braking. The braking distance depends on the surface of the roadway you're on, the weight of the vehicle, and other factors.

It might be helpful to know—maybe scary to know—that a typical tractor tailor rig, for instance, traveling at 55 miles an hour, calculating for perception time, reaction time, and braking distance, takes more than 500 feet to stop, from the time the driver first determines that he needs to stop.

We use calculations like these in accident reconstruction, including a case we had in Goldsboro. Our client was going to work in the morning. She pulled out from a stop sign onto a main street and was struck after three or four seconds by a law enforcement vehicle that was traveling 100 miles an hour at impact. Ironically, it was on its way to a wreck.

Our accident reconstruction expert downloaded the black box from the law enforcement vehicle to show the speed at impact and the approach speed. It showed the driver's acceleration and braking, or lack thereof. This reconstructionist calculated that when our client pulled out from the stop sign, the law enforcement vehicle was about 600 feet away from the point of impact.

Then, taking into account perception/reaction time and the danger zone, our human factors expert was able to provide us with testimony that he would have been outside of our client's danger zone, maybe even outside of her visibility altogether. At the least, if he had been visible, he would have been so far back that it would have been within a "safe" distance.

That information was vital in helping us to secure a good settlement for our client, a wonderful woman who had suffered some serious orthopedic injuries.

There's one other factor I want to mention in preventing accidents, and that's adjusting to driving conditions. Here in North Carolina, we seldom have an ice storm or a snow storm, but when we do, I'm always surprised at the calls I get after such a storm from people who lost control of their vehicle. People typically tell me that they were driving the speed limit, but because of the snow, they lost control of their vehicle. The law in North Carolina, and I believe in almost every state, is that while you have a duty to observe the speed limit, you have a further duty to drive at a speed that's safe considering all the surrounding circumstances including weather, roadway, visibility, et cetera.

In other words, what might be a lawful speed on a clear day would be a negligently high speed on a foggy day when your visibility is extremely limited. I hear this too often from defendants in our cases or even from my own clients, so my message is this: We always have to not only be aware of the speed limit, but also to drive at a reasonably safe speed, even if that's less than the speed limit, depending on the weather conditions and the roadway conditions and our visibility, like after dark, when you just can't see as well.

Okay, end of accident prevention message. Let's assume that despite driving as safely as you can, you still find yourself in an auto accident. Here's what you need to know.

What You Should Know if You Are in an Accident

Most people understand the basics of a minor collision: pull over to a safe place if possible, check everyone for injuries, call 9-1-1, and exchange information with the other driver. More serious incidents can get more complicated.

If you're injured in an accident, the first thing you need to do is seek appropriate medical help. That's usually going to be taken care of by EMTs or first responders on the scene. If you've got visible injuries and you can't get out of your vehicle, they're going to get you to an emergency room somewhere.

Sometimes injuries don't manifest themselves immediately at the accident scene. Maybe due to the rush of adrenaline from the shock of a collision, or for other reasons, sometimes symptoms don't become apparent until a little later after the wreck.

People may not be appear to be seriously injured at the scene, and may not even think at that point they need medical help, but sometimes you can have a soft tissue injury, like a cervical strain or sprain—whiplash is a common one—that shows up in the next day or so. That's something to be aware of as you go on after the accident.

Documenting Your Case

If you're not badly hurt, and you're able, try to talk to any witnesses or people who come to render assistance at the scene. They may be able to offer some important information about the wreck. The investigating officer may or may not take note of the witnesses' statements and contact information, so gathering information yourself can be helpful. Use your cell phone to take a picture of them. Sometimes I get into these cases six months later, and I'm told there were plenty of witnesses, but no one obtained their contact information. We try to track them down, but most of the time we're not able to find them so long after the fact. So it's important to document as much as you can at the scene.

Take pictures of anything that you feel is important: the damage to your car, the location of the vehicles after the wreck, the other driver's information. Take pictures of visible injuries, for instance when you've got glass all over your face or you've got a cut. I always tell people, with regard to scars or any kind of disfigurement, it's important to get pictures early just to show how bad it was. It's also important to take pictures of what it looks like once it's healed because that's what you will live with. It may look atrocious the first 30 days, but it may clear up and not look as bad after that.

In the aftermath of the accident, seek medical help if you need it. I never encourage people to seek medical help unnecessarily or to run up the medical bill, but suppose you're in a wreck, and let's say your neck hurts a little and your back hurts a little. Maybe you just don't want to go to the hospital, and you really think you're going to be okay, but if the symptoms do persist for a few days, then seek some medical help and at least get it documented that you have complained about your neck or back or whatever the specific injury is.

All too frequently, I see insurance companies take advantage of a delay in treatment. They'll argue to me or to the unrepresented claimant that they must not have been hurt too badly, if at all, since that they did not seek medical help immediately. They turned down the ambulance when the police officer offered it. They didn't go to the doctor that night. The longer you go without treatment, the more you're arming the insurance company with some argument that perhaps you weren't hurt in the wreck, that maybe something happened later that caused you to show up in an emergency room or in your doctor's office. That is sad, but true.

I always encourage people not to seek unnecessary medical treatment or incur unnecessary medical expenses, but on the other hand, I also say, if there were ever a time in your life to err on the side of caution—on the side of being treated versus not being treated—it's an automobile accident for which somebody else is responsible. I would encourage people to err on the side of getting treatment within a reasonably short period of time, if not immediately.

When you do seek treatment, remember that doctors are going to record their history of what you tell them about what happened, so be careful and accurate about it. If it were a stop sign, you don't want to say that somebody ran through a traffic light and hit you. That's an inconsistency that a defense lawyer will one day point out in your medical records. The things you tell your doctors are going to be in their medical records. They are not going to remember you or what you specifically told them except for how that is reflected in their notes. So you have to be careful about that. If it's your right shoulder that's hurt, make sure that you note it as your right shoulder, not your left shoulder.

In a perfect world, we would be able to listen to our doctors dictate their notes and know right away if they get something wrong, but we don't. It's really hard later to rebut any fact that is in the doctors' notes. There's even a theory of law that says you can really rely on what people tell their doctors because they're trying to get help. They've got a health issue, and if they're going to ever tell the truth at all, this is when they will tell the truth.

There's a balancing act in this. In your medical records, you don't want to sound like you're a complainer, a whiner, or exaggerator of your symptoms. At the same time, if you're not careful, and you don't list a symptom, or you don't mention it right away, and then it shows up in the records a month later for the first time, insurance companies are going to be very skeptical of that. I always encourage my clients, while keeping a positive attitude, to make sure the doctor knows every symptom. If you're having headaches, mention them. If your foot hurts, mention it. If your knee hurts, mention it.

What I have found is that sometimes when there is an acute or serious orthopedic injury, you may overlook any less significant injuries in your complaints. For example, suppose you have crushed your right shoulder. As that right shoulder heals, you start to mention your toes hurting, or your foot, or some other unrelated body part, so you've got to be careful.

I have sometimes even seen mild brain injuries going undiagnosed, or untreated, or even undetected early on, when there is another fairly serious, acute injury. Then as your acute injury begins to heal, it becomes more apparent to those around you, and maybe even to you, that there is something not right. The patient, though, is often not the first to perceive a mild brain injury.

In a typical scenario, I'll be talking to a client, saying, "Well, it looks like you're not in a walker anymore, you got out of the wheelchair. You went to the walker, now you're out of the walker, and you're doing a whole lot better," and the client starts telling me things like, "Yeah, but I don't know when I'll be able to go back to work." "Why?" "I just don't think I can do my job, and I just don't know what to do. There is something wrong and I am not sure what it is"

The most typical mild brain injury symptoms are blurred vision and headaches, but other symptoms of mild brain injuries can be subtle. They can include having difficulty organizing yourself the way you could before you had that injury. One of my clients described it for me as being "a little discombobulated." You can't put your finger on exactly what it is, but you can't read the newspaper like you used to; maybe you have difficulty getting organized at work if you have a multitasking job. You're a little more irritable. You have wide mood swings. You might be laughing one minute and crying the next.

It's usually a person's significant other or some of their coworkers who can identify those symptoms. Someone who doesn't know this person very well might not even detect that anything is wrong. Your doctors have been trying to fix the obvious problem of the acute orthopedic injury, and the whole time you may have this other injury that up until this point isn't even showing up in your medical records. This happens more often than you'd think.

So if there's a concussion or any loss of consciousness, no matter how slight, it needs to be checked out. Gaps in memory can be a clue. I had a client who insisted that she had not lost consciousness. I asked her, "What's the first thing that you remember after the accident?" And she said, "Well, I remember there was emergency personnel, an EMT person knocking on my window and they wanted to get me out of the car." Well, that probably happened at least 10 minutes after the wreck. Those gaps in memory sometimes make it easier to identify a loss of consciousness than just simply asking the question. I sometimes think that doctors are perhaps not as sensitive to that as we plaintiff's lawyers are, because they're so focused on trying to fix the apparent problem, the acute problem.

Along with all of the medical records, there are other aspects to documenting your case. If you miss time from work because of the accident, you can recover your lost wages, but the insurance company does not just accept your word of what you lost in income. The easiest way to prove income is when you're working for a company and you're either paid by the hour, or the week, or month. They can issue a statement of how long you were out and what your gross pay would have been during that period. On the other hand, if you're self-employed and you're out of work a month, you've got to document and support your claim for loss of income. You've got to be prepared, for example, to produce your last year's tax returns.

Also, if you use sick leave or personal time off (PTO), and are paid because of that benefit, it is still a loss to you and a part of your claim.

You also need to document personal property that might have been lost. If you had a laptop in your car that was destroyed in the wreck, get all your paperwork for that. If you had tools in your car that were either lost or stolen, the better you can document that loss, the more likely you are to be able to recover the cost of your loss.

Dealing with Property Damage

When I refer to property damage with regard to an auto accident, what I mean is the damage to the vehicle. One of the first questions I ask when someone calls is, "Were you able to drive your vehicle after the wreck?" If they were not, then "Have you had an estimate done? Do you know what it's going to cost to repair the vehicle?" Sometimes I'm told that the car was totaled. Then I need to know the make and year of the car as well as its features. It takes a lot less impact to total a 20-year-old car than a brand new car because the car is totaled when the cost of the repair is more than the car's value.

When a car is totaled, the claimant is entitled to the reasonable fair market value of the car. That's as if it would be sitting on a used car lot somewhere, not its value to you. Often, sadly, I see older cars that have a lot of mileage on them, but are absolutely dependable to the owner. Then the car gets totaled and may only be worth a few hundred dollars. Sometimes it does go the other way, and the car is actually worth more than the person paid for it maybe six months earlier. If you have a car that is totaled shortly after you bought it, whether you bought it new or used, the best evidence of its value when it was purchased, is what you paid for it. So your purchase records are important in the event that your vehicle becomes totaled.

Insurance companies focus almost immediately on the amount of damage to the vehicle. If the damage is barely visible—suppose you got tapped or had a rear-ender—and there's only one little indentation, then I probably would not take that case. I would also want to warn that person to avoid going out and running up medical bills on the assumption that they're going to be covered by the claim. The less visible the property damage, the more difficult it is to settle that claim, especially if there is a whole lot of medical treatment.

There was a study done many years ago where the researchers surveyed juries hearing wreck cases. The study determined that the number one thing the juries wanted to see was the pictures of the vehicle involved. They were asking the question: "Is it reasonable to think that a person in this vehicle could have sustained the injuries that this plaintiff is presenting to us?" You run into some skeptical jurors with that.

Securing a Rental Car

Sometimes the first thing out of a client's mouth is, "I need to get a rental." I think it's important for claimants to know that you're entitled to the loss of use of your car if it's not drivable, for every day you're without the use of your car. Even when your car is totaled, you're entitled to loss of use for every day until they make you a reasonable offer for the replacement value of your car. You're entitled to the loss of use of your vehicle whether or not you use that money to rent a car. I think the knee jerk reaction is, "Get me into a rental," but I always caution my clients to think about whether they really need one. If you've broken your right foot, for example, you can't drive, although you may need a rental for people to be able to take you to the doctor or something.

You may also have a second vehicle that you can use while your car is not drivable. There may be another alternative for you, rather than a rental car, and since you're going to get paid as if you had a rental, that could mean a little more cash to you in a settlement. My advice is not to rent a car unless you absolutely need one.

I always caution my clients to begin the process of looking for a replacement vehicle as soon as we know that their car is being totaled. Don't wait until you hear what they're going to pay you for your car, because once you get that figure, you're also going to be given only a short period of time to return your rental vehicle.

I usually encourage clients to go back to the same dealer, or the same finance company, especially if they are upside down on the car, meaning that the value of the car is less than what is owed on it. When your upside-down car is totaled completely because of someone else's bad choice, that's a bad situation, but if you've been making your monthly payments, and you go to your same finance company, they'll probably be willing to finance the new one, also upside down. That's just a little piece of practical advice.

Evaluating Your Claim

One of the typical questions I get asked early on, sometimes even in the first meeting with a client, is "What's my case worth?" There's no way in the world that I, or anyone else, can know the answer to that until you have fully recovered from your injuries. The medical/legal term for that is reaching MMI—maximum medical improvement—and the reason is that you never want to settle a claim with any big uncertainties about the future.

Now, there may be some uncertainty, but you try to tie it down as much as you can with a doctor. Suppose, for example, that I have that client who was in a wheelchair, then using a walker, then walking with a cane, and maybe now is walking without a cane, so the doctor releases him from treatment. I'm going to want to know two things from the doctor: one, is he as good as he's going to get, and two, what kind of permanent impairment or residual problem is he going to have. That's usually expressed as some type of percentage impairment. In this case, he's going to have, for example, 10 percent impairment to his left lower extremity for the rest of his life.

Your age also determines the value of that. If you're 20 and you have 10 percent impairment, that situation is certainly much more compensable than if you're 75 with 10 percent impairment. That's notwithstanding the fact that the older we get, the more valuable our health is.

I am particularly conscious of injuries that affect a claimant or a client's ability to ambulate. In my opinion, that may even be the measure of our health as we get older, not so much the typical measures like blood pressure or sugar level. I think our ability to get around—to be on our feet for an hour to shop at Christmas, to walk from the parking lot, to stand in line, to go on a cruise, to do whatever—defines our quality of life as much as anything. To me, any injury that affects your ability to ambulate, particularly if it's a permanent effect, enhances the value of your loss, which likewise increases the value of what a settlement should be.

In assessing the value of your claim, we look at not only lasting impairment but also anticipated future medical expenses. In cases with serious injuries I retain the services of a medical life-care planner, who determines and meets with all the treating doctors about what the patient is going to need going forward.

For example, I'm working on a motorcycle accident case. Our client lost his right foot and about four inches of his leg. He was a construction worker, so his lifetime earnings have been affected. He's been fitted with a prosthesis for that right foot, but that gets into a life-care plan because while prosthetics are better made now, they still don't last forever. He's going to have it replaced, and prosthetics require certain ongoing examinations, kind of like blood work.

He's also going to need handicapped mechanisms in his vehicle. He's not going to be able to brake or accelerate with his right foot. He's going to have to learn to use hand instruments or left foot braking and acceleration. His vehicle will need to be handicap-equipped. All of these things get factored into his life-care plan.

Evaluating your case is always tough, even when I have all of the information. I have the past medical bills; I have a handle on the expected future medical bills. I account for lost income and loss of future income, if that applies. I also look at what I call the loss of quality of life. That's not a statutory element of damages, but physical pain and mental suffering are, and I believe that is part of the mental suffering.

For example, if you want to go see your grandchild play at a sporting event and you can't, because you're not able to sit in the stands, that may not cause you physical pain, but it is mental anguish. It is a loss in the quality of your life, resulting from your accident. That aspect of an injury case can sometimes be really hard for juries to understand and accept. Having a "blackboard" is easier: past medical expenses, future medical expenses, lost wages. When you start getting into physical pain and mental suffering, you sometimes lose some of our more conservative jurors.

Some clients will come to me with a preconceived idea of how much their case is worth. They may say, "Well, Mr. Whitley, I'm not going to take anything less than $100,000." I usually ask them what they base that number on. Do they have experience in evaluating claims? Has somebody told them that? Odds are, it's just a number they grabbed out of the sky.

The truth is that an attorney like me will know much more than the typical claimant will know about the value of his or her claim. You wouldn't hire an electrician and think that you know more about installing some switches and putting in wiring than he would know. You trust that he knows what he's doing. I sometimes have to remind my clients that I should and do know more than they do about what a case is worth.

Some factors affect the value of your claim, like the risk of contributory negligence. Maybe you lack an ability to articulate your losses to a jury. Maybe a jury is put off by your appearance. There are outside factors as well that can affect the value of a case. Here in North Carolina, for instance, we have a conservative jury pool and you can't always count on getting what you should get.

All these things play into differentiating the value of your loss, but I always make it clear to my clients that there's one thing I don't know more about than they do, and that is the day-to-day effect of their injury on them and their lives. I can read their medical records, and I can get to know them very well, but they're the only ones who really know the full effect of their injury.

When I meet with a client, one of my favorite ways to begin is to tell them, "All right. We're going to write a paper, and the subject of the paper is going to be, 'I wish this accident hadn't happened because . . .' and now I want you to tell me every reason in the world that you wish this hadn't happened." I'm trying to get from them things that you wouldn't ordinarily pick up, like, "I can't reach my arm around my back to put on my bra in the morning," or "When I get out of the car, I have to reach over and open the door with my right hand because I can't use my left arm." I want to know the things that no one who hadn't been through it would really know. Those are things you won't pick up from a medical record, and that's why I always tell them that they know more about their loss and their injury and the effect on their lives than I do.

In the end, there is almost always a difference between the value of your loss and the value of your claim. You can never really make up for what you have lost. Think of my client who lost his foot. How much money would make him say, "Okay, well, that was worth it. You know, I lost my foot, but I got enough money that it's even."? That just doesn't happen.

One last note about automobile accident cases: We've been talking here about cases in which you retain a lawyer to represent you and deal with the insurance company. If it's a smaller case, and you are dealing with the insurance company yourself, there is still one time you should definitely check with a lawyer, and that's when the adjuster tells you what they're willing to pay you. Is it within a reasonable range? If you don't ask anyone, and you rely on what that adjuster is telling you your case is worth, you're relying on the very company that's going to be paying you the money. Before you decide to accept that amount, you need another opinion from someone who doesn't have a vested interest in the outcome.

The Trial from Hell: Rose's Story

I told you in the last chapter about my trial from heaven, so I guess it's only fair I should also share the trial from hell—the one where everything, except the verdict, that could go wrong went wrong. My client—I'll call her Rose—was a hospice nurse in her early 40s. While on her job, on her way to a home visit, she was rear-ended by a commercial truck. It was a bad wreck, and Rose sustained what was later diagnosed as mild brain injury. She was not able to go back to her beloved profession; in fact, when we concluded the case, she hadn't been able to go back to any kind of gainful employment, but otherwise, she was doing reasonably well.

One of the things that happens with a brain injury is that it becomes difficult for the injured person to retrieve words, and a result of that they get tired easily. It's kind of a mystery to them and to people who know them, because they're not working, they're staying home, and yet they need to take a two-hour nap in the middle of the day because they're just worn out. It's because simple, everyday conversation wears them out. It can be hard for us to grasp that because when we talk and respond our brain isn't normally working very hard. We might occasionally struggle a moment to pull out a word, but they have that struggle almost with every word they say. Their speech is slower because they have to reach for the words. That was one of Rose's symptoms.

Wide mood swings are another symptom of brain injury, and Rose certainly had those. She would become tearful easily, and you never knew what would trigger her.

The injured person may have trouble recognizing the symptoms of their own injury. With a mild brain injury, it's people who knew them before the injury who will recognize a change in them, or notice that they seem a little bit off. It's more difficult for them to be organized, or to structure things. They may have difficulty concentrating or reading. I've had mildly brain injured clients tell me sometimes that they used to read the paper front to back every morning, and now they can't even get through any one article. They can't stay focused. They may also become sensitive to sounds and flashing lights, to the point where it's even difficult for them to watch TV.

Rose had all these symptoms but her claim was hotly contested because there was no visible physical damage to her brain. That's often the case with a mild brain injury. A more severe brain injury is almost always accompanied by some physical damage to the brain that can be seen with a CAT scan or an MRI or some other objective means. What I've learned from the doctors over the years is that any bleeding in the brain or trauma to the brain kills brain cells. If there are not a lot of these dead cells, the injury may not show up in an MRI or a CAT scan. One doctor explained it to me this way: "There was a time when we couldn't see some of the planets because we didn't have powerful enough telescopes and now we do. We're probably going to have even more powerful telescopes and see things in the future that we can't see now, and the same thing is true in medicine. One day we'll probably have equipment that will allow us to see these small, damaged, or dead brain cells, but we don't have that equipment now."

We had to try the case and it was in a small town in the middle of nowhere. It wasn't close to any big city, and there were no good hotels, so I was commuting two hours each way, every day of the trial.

I knew it was going to be a challenging trial, so as we began jury selection, I decided to use some of the ideas I recently had been learning from jury consultants.

One of the things that we were taught in law school, as trial lawyers, was to avoid "poisoning" the jury pool by mentioning any difficult subjects out loud so that everybody could hear.

But what we're taught today, by the best jury consultants, is just the opposite of that. You need to be able to talk about any prejudices that some people might have about lawsuits or about lawyers or about trying to recover money. This was really one of the first trials where I used this new training.

In fact—I won't forget this—I started out by turning to the jury without notes. I spread my legs and my arms and looked at them and said something like, "Ladies and gentlemen, we read a whole lot about lawsuits. We read about cases and big sums of money and jackpot justice and we hear about frivolous lawsuits. We hear people say that there are too many lawsuits. We even hear people say that lawyers are messing up the whole system." I went on for a bit and then I just turned and said, "I'm really interested in hearing what each one of you has to say about that. Mr. Smith, juror number 11, do you have any comments?"

It was two or three hours later before I asked my next question. That's what we've been taught lately, that is, to get the jury to talk. In the past, we lawyers liked to do all the talking and you'd say, "Anybody disagree?" You'd almost stifle them. Now you've got to get them to talk.

You just work at trying to get them to talk. Then you also give them permission to take a position that they might think is contrary to your position. You might remember John Edwards, the guy who ran for president. He was a great trial lawyer notwithstanding his shortcomings in his personal life. One of the things he would do was start by saying, "Even my momma thinks there are too many lawsuits." What he was doing was giving the jurors permission to take that position. Once you get that first person, when somebody does say, "Well, Mr. Whitley, I have to admit, I think that there are probably too many lawsuits and there are certainly too many frivolous lawsuits," then you can turn to another juror and say, "What do you think about that? Do you agree with that?"

You can also suggest that some people think there should be a limit to the amount of recovery or the amount of the damages for pain and suffering. It's another "My momma thinks that . . ." kind of statement. You can go on to say there are other people who think that there really shouldn't be a limit and you should get whatever your particular injury calls for. Then you ask a juror, "Which of those two thoughts do you most agree with or disagree with?" The whole goal is just to get people talking. The more they talk, the more you can learn in order to best use your challenges.

So with my new method, jury selection in Rose's case was taking a lot longer than normal. On the second or third day, the judge developed a tooth abscess and had to be excused.

We got a replacement judge who was a little harder on me and the way I was questioning the jury. He tried to rush me along.

Then we ran out of jurors. They got to talking so much that their opinions were easy to see. With those you don't want, you try to get them to agree that they're probably not going to change their opinion about this limitation on pain and suffering, even if the judge tells them that there is no limitation. Then you can excuse them for cause and you don't have to use one of your peremptory challenges.

Anyway, we ran out of jurors, so the new judge ordered the sheriff to go out and pick up 20-30 people from Walmart—yes, Walmart. We finally got our 12-person jury and they, at least those who had been shopping at Walmart, were not happy jurors. It was around Thanksgiving and we only worked two days Thanksgiving week, so we were out those three days. The following week, after a day or two back, a tornado came through the county, though not the town itself. But when you're having a jury trial, you have jurors from all over the county, not just the city you're in, so we were delayed again because a lot of the jurors couldn't come in.

Trying the case seemed like it was going to be a lost cause because the other side brought in some really outstanding experts, people who had written books on brain injuries. They were trying to show that Rose just didn't have a serious brain injury at all. They acknowledged that she had been hurt a little, but they argued that with a brain injury in the first year or so any change is always an improvement. Their expert testified that she wouldn't have been getting better for a couple of months and then start getting worse so soon.

They brought in an expert from Kentucky. When they asked if he had any first impressions of the case, he said,

"Yeah, I looked at the very first record on the file." It was the report from the EMS at the accident scene. When they first got to Rose, they gave her the questions for the Glasgow Coma Scale (GCS), which is a tool to assess brain injury. She had scored a perfect 15 on the GCS, and you usually don't do that if you have a brain injury of any kind. So that wasn't a great start with that expert.

Then they brought in another Chapel Hill neuropsychiatrist who had tested her and said that he didn't think there was anything wrong with her.

Finally, after what seemed like an endless trial, we got to a jury verdict, and it was a very pleasant surprise. It was a favorable verdict, maybe the largest verdict they'd had in that county. The verdict was $500,000 and I remember thinking it was a miracle, but I'll always remember it as the trial from hell. It was just a horrible experience; I think it was because of all the experts from the other side and my commuting two hours a day. But I was glad for our client and I believed my client; I never bought into the argument that she didn't have a brain injury, and apparently the jury didn't either, or they would have never given her that kind of money for her claim.

Chapter 5: More Driving Lessons: Bigger and Badder

SOME OF the most devastating accident cases I see are trucking accidents. Tractor-trailer wrecks are always worse in terms of power and energy and injuries. Unfortunately, many of them result in fatalities. They are much different from other motor vehicle accidents, and so I want to talk about them separately.

First of all, if you have been hurt in a serious trucking accident, you need a lawyer to represent you, and you need to make sure that the lawyer you hire has specific experience in trucking accidents. Lots of lawyers say they do, but some of their experience is minimal.

What Makes Trucking Accidents Different

That experience is critical because there are extensive rules and regulations that apply to tractor-trailers that do not apply to ordinary passenger vehicles. You need an attorney who is familiar with the Federal Motor Carrier Regulations that govern interstate trucking and interstate commerce. These rules and regulations apply to every aspect of trucking. They govern the trucking companies, the vehicles, and the drivers.

The reason that there are more rules and regulations on tractor-trailers and their drivers is that they're naturally much more dangerous. Tractor-trailers are always on interstate highways, or at least more typically traveling on interstate highways than city roads. The speed limits are greater; the vehicles are traveling faster; they're heavier. They're driven many more miles in the course of a year. They cross state lines. They have a much greater stopping distance than a passenger car, when you take into account the perception time, reaction time, and braking time.

And that trucker who's at the wheel has probably been on the road perhaps all day as opposed to the guy who's just driving to Raleigh for an hour and a half. It's a tough life for a driver. You don't eat healthily. You don't sleep regularly and structurally. The job just lends itself to poor health.

Because of all that, getting your commercial driver's license is much more complicated, complex, and difficult than getting an ordinary driver's license.

A commercial driver undergoes much more thorough testing, including a written test and a driving test. The driver has to undergo a medical exam and routinely meet specific medical requirements. Anything that can affect the driver's fatigue or physical and mental capacity is regulated and documented.

In the Department of Transportation (DOT) medical exam that they have to undergo, they're asked questions about their health, about their vision, their hearing, diabetes, blood pressure, and health history. To a large extent, the drivers fill out that medical report themselves. Then they certify that what they have put in that report is true and that they recognize that providing false information would disqualify them from obtaining a commercial driver's license.

In a lot of my cases against trucking companies, I find that the medical exams become pretty perfunctory. I'm not sure these drivers realize the implications when they're signing off on these forms, because they often don't provide truthful information.

When a truck operator is hired, the company has to keep an employee file. They have to do background checks on the employee, mainly for things that would disqualify him as a driver, like a driving-while-impaired charge while he is operating a commercial vehicle. They also track the driver's medical check-ups. Conditions like diabetes, high blood pressure, or sleep apnea may not disqualify a commercial driver, but that driver will have to be tested more frequently and may have restrictions in operating a commercial vehicle.

The drivers and the trucking companies are also required to do preventive maintenance and inspection of the trucks. Every time they start a trip in the morning, a tractor-trailer driver is under a regulatory duty to have a safety inspection of his vehicle, including the wheels, the brakes, and all the things that would be important for safe operation of that truck. I often find that truckers don't do that as rigorously as they should, but nevertheless, it is a rule.

The company that hires the truck driver is responsible for that driver, and they're also responsible for their drivers following all of the Federal Motor Carrier Regulations. They're not able to claim they didn't know that a driver was not medically qualified. It's their responsibility to know and they're going to be held accountable just as the driver would.

The Sisters Foster

A few years ago, I had a case that really illustrates how difficult and devastating these tractor-trailer wrecks can be.

This accident happened in Kinston. There were two older women, the Foster sisters, and an older fellow, a family friend, who was riding with them. The sisters were in their early 70s. They were going to the beauty parlor, which was at the community college because the cosmetic school there provided that service in their training.

One of the sisters was driving, and they came up to a busy intersection. It's probably the most complicated intersection in the whole town of Kinston; all of the roadways that converge there are pretty busy and multi-lane. They were going to make a left turn, to head east. Theirs was the second or third car in line at the light when they got the green turn signal. As they were going through the intersection, they were literally run over by a tractor-trailer that was heading north. It just ran right over them. All three were killed immediately; their bodies were dismembered. The police photos were the worst I had ever seen, or have seen since.

The supervisor of the first responders in the county told me it was the worst wreck that he had ever been to or heard about. In fact, one of the first responders was brand new to the job. It was her first wreck, and she resigned right after. That was it for her.

The reason it was so brutal was that this tractor-trailer was probably going anywhere from 45 to 55 miles an hour at impact. When it crashed into this little four-door car, it didn't just push it out of the way. It went over the top and crushed it. It was an unusual angle of impact, and that's what resulted in the horrendous deaths.

I'll never forget these ladies' children telling me that they weren't able to say good-bye and they weren't able to open the coffin and they weren't absolutely sure that within their specific coffin was all of the remains of their mom. This was a wonderful, ordinary, middle class family in Kinston. Their parents had worked all their lives. They were all working people, and they really bonded during the months and years after the wreck. The family came together in the absence of their mother hen. That truck had killed fine Kinston people and it all could have been avoided. This was my backyard and I did not like it!

Over the years, I've learned that in wrongful death cases generally, the family members want to know what happened and they need to know what happened to begin to get some closure. In this case, they knew what happened. They didn't know all of the graphic details, but they knew enough. And they knew that both coffins were closed at the funerals.

In police photographs from the site, the truck driver can be seen walking around, looking fairly normal. He declined any medical assistance at first—he signed a form—but then within 30 minutes, or maybe an hour, he started showing signs of a stroke. His lips drooped, and he was taken to the hospital, where he was actually diagnosed with a stroke.

In the law, a sudden and unanticipated medical emergency is one of the defenses for a person who causes an accident. I've run into that a few times over the years, and I've never really seen one that was legitimate.

The trucking company in this particular case relied on that sudden medical emergency defense and so it became crucial for me to get into the driver's medical history. While the defense is always entitled to all of the medical records, past and present, for the plaintiff who's claiming an injury that resulted from the wreck, the plaintiff is not normally entitled to the defendant's medical records unless it's a case of driving while impaired. I had to go through his employee file, go through all of his DOT medical exams that were available, and depose two different doctors. One was his treating doctor, in Virginia, and the other was the DOT examiner, who was a North Carolina doctor.

These trucking companies often create a relationship with a medical facility, or a doctor, or a PA, and they get better rates for all the truckers who get their medical exams there. So the motor carrier medical exam is performed by someone other than the driver's primary care doctor.

When these truckers fill out their medical exam, there are questions about sleeping disorders like sleep apnea, which is common among truck drivers. The form asks if you snore loudly. This driver, like almost every truck driver, answered no. Remember, when they sign this, it's like swearing under oath that all this information is true. When I went up to Virginia and took the deposition of his primary care doctor to get his medical history, I also deposed his wife. She happened to mention that they had separate bedrooms. I just took a leap of faith and said, "Well, I bet you sleep separately because of his loud snoring, don't you?" She said, "Yes, that's exactly the reason." Loud snoring, of course, is a common symptom of sleep apnea.

We argued that this accident was probably due to driver fatigue and that the stroke was coincidental after the wreck.

There were witnesses who described the truck driver's operation a mile or two leading up to the intersection; some described him as being in a daze. He didn't look right. The neurologist I consulted about the stroke symptoms said that it was sleep deprivation. We've all had that experience of temporarily nodding off, where all of a sudden you just catch yourself. But when it happens behind the wheel it's extremely dangerous. And it's something that will keep happening until you get some real rest. So the lesson to us all is to stop and get some rest before we get back on the road.

Driver fatigue is very common among truck drivers, even though they are restricted as to how many hours they can drive in a 24-hour period. They are required to keep logs to document their driving hours. What I have learned, though, is that the industry often cheats on those logs. Drivers get pushed by the trucking companies. If it takes them longer to get somewhere and deliver their cargo, then the company's not making as much money, so drivers are tempted to speed, take shortcuts, and exceed their hours of operation.

Since the trucking company was arguing it was a sudden medical emergency, we also worked to show that this stroke was certainly not unanticipated. He was overweight, as most truck drivers are, and in fact, the police photos showed that there was a sugar measuring device in his cab. We learned that he had diabetes. I suspected that he also had sleep apnea, based on what his wife had told me about his snoring.

We contended that the trucking company knew or should have known about his medical capacity or lack of capacity. They would be responsible because he's their agent. The case was eventually settled in mediation, about two years after the wreck, and the resolution did help to bring some closure to the family.

One of the things I learned from that case—not that I hadn't learned it before, but it was so clear in this case—is how much we want for our loved ones to have a peaceful death when their time comes. I realized that the one comforting piece of information that I could share with the family was that these deaths had been instantaneous. Their mom and aunt probably didn't even know it happened.

It makes me think about families where a family member has been violently killed in a criminal act or terrorism or something that brutalizes the human being. I think it can become a permanent mar on the memories they have of that loved one. The memory of the way they died can make it much harder to recall the good times. As I've gotten older and more experienced, especially with death cases, I've come to see that's one of the things families dread most in an automobile accident or a trucking wreck.

The Foster sisters' case does illustrate how important it is for a lawyer who's handling a trucking case to be familiar with the Federal Motor Carrier Regulations. I started as a young lawyer taking seminars from experienced trucking lawyers to learn every aspect of dealing with these regulations. A family lawyer or someone who only handles fender-benders will not be equipped to handle a trucking case.

Chapter 6: Insurance 101

WE'VE TALKED a lot in this book about insurance companies, mostly from my perspective as an opposing lawyer. But we should also talk some about insurance from the consumer perspective.

It may seem strange, but I find that most people are fairly clueless about what insurance coverage they have. Then when they're in an accident, they discover too late that they don't have enough insurance, or the right kind of coverage to protect their interest. Here's my motto: Know before you need to. It's like a will—once you need it, it's too late.

Know Before You Need To

Do you know what coverage you have? If you're not sure, take a look at your policy and go to what's called the declarations page, or dec page. It will show the nature of your various coverages, like bodily injury (also called liability), medical payment, collision, property damage, underinsured, and underinsured. It will show which coverages you have in your policy and the amount of each coverage.

If you're not able to locate your policy or you have trouble understanding it, call your insurance agent. They should have your policy on file and can answer any questions about your coverages.

The more important coverage on an automobile policy is the liability portion. That's the amount that is available in the event that you cause injury to another person. The coverage is usually expressed as a per person amount and a per accident amount. Every state requires some kind of liability coverage, although the minimum amount varies from state to state. North Carolina requires $30,000 bodily injury liability per person, $60,000 bodily liability per accident, and $25,000 property damage. On the dec page you may see liability written as 30/60. That means that no one person can get more than $30,000 from an accident and no one accident will be paid at more than $60,000, regardless of how many people are injured.

On any policy that is more than the minimum, you will usually see amounts for uninsurance and underinsurance. It is typically written for the same amount as the liability coverage. For example, if you've got 100/300 liability coverage on your automobile policy, you probably also have 100/300 in underinsurance and in uninsurance.

Uninsurance protects you in the event you are injured by a motorist who is literally uninsured. As in the example above, suppose you have 100/300 coverage and you are injured by someone who has no insurance at all. Then you will have 100/300 available to you through your uninsurance coverage, and your company will treat you the same as if you were a stranger to your policy.

Underinsurance works similarly, but it comes into play when the responsible driver does not have enough insurance to cover your damages. Using the same example of you having 100/300 underinsurance coverage, suppose you are injured and your claim is found to be worth $100,000 but the person who injured you has only $50,000 coverage. The underinsurance in your policy would kick in the difference, so you would have the $100,000 to cover your claim, $50,000 from the at-fault driver and $50,000 from your own underinsurance.

Underinsurance has been around a long time, but people seem to know even less about that than they do about their liability coverage. One important thing you should know about underinsurance is that it protects you <u>and</u> any family member who lives with you. So if you have a child and they're in somebody else's car, your underinsurance is going to follow them to that car if it's needed.

If there are two related adults who live in the same household with separate policies, then the underinsurance for each one of them would apply to the other. For example, let's say a brother and sister live together and they each have 100/300 on their respective individual policies. If either one is hurt by someone who is underinsured, there would be $200,000 available in underinsurance, because you can stack underinsurance from members of your household if they're related to you by blood or marriage.

There's one other coverage that is not well-known, and I always recommend it to my clients. That's <u>medical payment coverage</u>, also called med pay. This is coverage you can buy with your automobile policy or with your homeowners' policy that will cover medical bills, regardless of fault. Med pay can come in handy, but insurance agents don't always tell their clients about it, even when they have it. Sometimes they tell our clients, even those who have med pay, that they should look to the party who was at fault.

Med pay coverage also follows you wherever you go. If I'm in your car, and we're in a wreck, whether it's your fault or another driver's fault. I would be able to collect the med pay that you have on your car, and if that's not enough to cover all of my medical bills, I could then stack or add my own med pay coverage to yours.

You can also have med pay on your homeowners' policy. Suppose I'm in your home as a guest, and I fall and get hurt. Let's say I've just had one too many glasses of wine and I fall down some steps. It's my fault; you as the homeowner have not done anything wrong. Med pay coverage, assuming you have it, and most homeowners' policies do, will cover my medical bills up to a certain amount.

When I'm meeting with a client who has been injured, they sometimes wonder why I ask about their insurance coverage, since they're not the one at fault. I need to know about all of the possible coverages that could apply. For instance, I always ask whether the responsible driver was also the owner of the car, or if they were driving somebody else's car. One of the basics of automobile insurance law is that the insurance on the vehicle is primary, and if you've got a non-owner driving and that person has coverage, then their liability coverage is secondary. That means you can add the two coverages. For example, suppose you and I each have $100,000 in liability coverage. If I borrow your car and happen to harm somebody while I'm driving it, your $100,000 policy would be first, and if that's exhausted, then they can go to my $100,000, if it's needed to compensate for the injury.

The Bottom Line on Insurance

Here's my advice: The best thing to do—when you read this book and before you or anyone you care about is involved in an accident of any kind—is to go meet with your insurance agent. Let them tell you what your coverage is, and explore whether you have enough coverage.

Recently, I spoke with a lady who was at fault in a wreck. She had received a letter from the other side, and wanted my advice. She only has $100,000 per person liability. She's a widow, she owns her house, and she owns a commercial building, so she's got assets, and they are at risk. The more assets you have, the more insurance you need to have. If you don't have enough insurance, but you do have assets, the other side can try to go after those assets and force you to liquidate them to pay a claim. If I have a client with a claim that's worth $100,000 and the responsible driver only has $50,000 in coverage, I'm going to find out what property, automobiles, et cetera, that individual owns because I may consider pursuing what is called an excess judgment against them. That means we would not just accept the $50,000 but demand that the insured individual pay some out of pocket. So it's important to make sure your assets are protected.

Get as much insurance as you can reasonably afford. Get a few quotes—you may be surprised at how inexpensive it can be to go from having 50/100 to having 300/500. You hope you'll never need it, but you'll be glad to have it if you do.

The Case for Insurance and Accident Reconstruction: Chase's Story

This case was unfolding as I started to write this book and was recently settled just in time to make it into the book. It was a motorcycle accident that happened on Thanksgiving Day, 2015.

At the time of the accident our client, Chase, was just 23 years old. He was riding his motorcycle from his girlfriend's house to his parents' house, traveling east on a narrow, two-lane rural road. The speed limit there was 55 miles per hour.

The defendant is another young man, Blake, who was going to his brother's house to fix a plumbing leak on Thanksgiving morning. He worked as a repairman and troubleshooter for his daddy's plumbing business and as part of his job, the company provided him a truck 24/7. He was always on call, and he could use that truck for any reason he chose. Blake was heading west on that same road until he stopped to turn left into his brother's driveway.

There was a witness driving behind Blake, and she stopped behind him. She was close to the center line, and she said she could see Chase approaching when all of a sudden Blake started his left turn, right in front of Chase's motorcycle. It was a bad, bad wreck.

A couple of Chase's friends and coworkers were among the volunteer first responders who came to the scene, not knowing that their friend was involved. Chase was so badly hurt that he was unrecognizable, but one of these first responders thought he recognized the bike and suspected that it might be Chase's. He saw a knapsack lying in the road where it had been thrown in the crash, and went through it looking for a license or registration to confirm that it was Chase.

The first responders didn't think Chase would even live to make it to the hospital, but somehow he did. He was in a coma for a couple of weeks. When Chase's family called us, about a month after the wreck, he was in Raleigh at Wake

Med Brain Injury Rehab Facility. It's part of the Wake Med hospital. I went there and met with his dad. Jimmy, his dad, brought me to Chase, who was in a private room, in an almost fetal position. His eyes were darting back and forth and looking at me in confusion. He was unable to communicate in any way. His dad introduced me to him, and that was my first moment with Chase.

He looked pretty pitiful. He had lost a lot of weight, and basically looked "out of it."

The family hired us to represent Chase in early January, about five weeks after the wreck. The first thing we did was obtain the accident report, and it looked fairly simple as far as who was at fault: Blake had turned in front of Chase's approaching motorcycle.

It's such a sad story. Chase was a young man with a bright future, but the accident left him with a brain injury that may require him to have care for the rest of his life. His parents wanted to care for him at home instead of in a facility, but insurance wouldn't cover the in-home care he needed, so they had to decide which of them would quit working to stay home with Chase. His dad quit his job and we had him declared Chase's guardian.

We had a life-care plan prepared, estimating Chase's needs for his projected lifetime. In the best case scenario, that life-care plan is about $8 million; in the worst case it's about $11 million, and he's going to need basically 24/7 care, at least to have somebody around, for the rest of his life.

We hired an economist to compute Chase's lifetime loss of earnings and the present value of the life-care plan.

Before the wreck, he had a good job and a decent income. He was a manager at a restaurant and had moved up in the organization. He was well-liked and well-respected. Our economist says he had the potential to have made more money than the typical high school graduate would make in a lifetime.

He had a girlfriend. They'd been together five years and planned to be married. He had been living at her house, with her, her mom, and her sister. They had asked him to move in after her dad's death a year earlier—the three women wanted to have a man around the house. And now he doesn't even remember her. The brain injury left gaps in his long-term and short-term memory, and their years together are just gone. Their relationship could not survive.

So in this case, we were dealing with a catastrophic injury, and also a commercial insurance policy, because the defendant was driving a company truck. The plumbing company had much more insurance coverage than most vehicles. The awful thing is, even though the plumbing company exercised due diligence and actually had more coverage than most small businesses have, it was still not enough to take care of Chase's needs.

Given the circumstances, I immediately obtained an engineer accident reconstructionist to analyze the wreck—to inspect the vehicles, go to the scene, make the measurements, and do an independent assessment. I've learned over the years the sooner you do that, the better. I've also learned that even when a case appears to be clear-cut, as this one did when I first saw the accident report, you never know. And this just happened to be one of those "you never know" times.

When I was talking to the insurance adjuster, I started to get suspicious, because she was doing a lot of hemming and hawing. She said that they had their own reconstructionist, that she wanted to get his conclusions, and she said there was some signs that Chase may have been speeding. We immediately filed suit.

The preliminary report from my accident reconstructionist described the incident as more of a head-on collision than a T-bone collision because the pickup was turning into the driveway at an angle, and the driveway itself was at an angle. Even though it was a very bad wreck, it was a fairly low-speed wreck. The reconstructionist agreed with what the trooper wrote on the accident report, which estimated Chase's approach speed at 55 mph and the impact speed at 45 mph.

In the meantime, I learned from the insurance company that their reconstructionist was saying that Chase's approach speed was about 81 mph, with an impact speed of 68 mph. The speed limit there is 55 mph, so if he were speeding, even though the truck had suddenly turned right in front of him, they could argue contributory negligence risking a zero recovery for Chase.

It's an example of the insurance company looking for anything they can to avoid paying and their hired expert was giving them some ammunition. For instance, the defendant driver's brother, the one whose home he was going to, of course heard the crash and came out of his house right away. He saw one of the first responders pick up Chase's knapsack that he had been wearing, and go through it, and then take it and put it in his truck. The brother thought that was very suspicious and shared it with the insurance company.

So the brother reported that to the insurance company, and it became "the mysterious knapsack evidence being secreted." I learned about that in deposing their accident reconstructionist. I subpoenaed all of his files, including emails, and the first email that came from the insurance company to him made some reference to "the knapsack that was taken away without law enforcement inspection."

Remember the first responder who was one of Chase's coworkers? He's the one who went through the knapsack, looking for a license to confirm that it was Chase, and he was standing right next to the highway patrol officer when he did it. That was how they identified Chase at the scene.

They were looking for anything they could to claim contributory negligence. Their reconstructionist claimed that Chase was speeding. His opinion was so different from our own expert that I hired a second expert to independently assess the speed. Our second expert agreed with our first expert and their opinion was that Chase's approach speed was 53–54 mph and his impact speed was 44–45 mph. That's hugely different from the 80 and 68 their expert was claiming, so we went to work to debunk his theory.

Everyone who knows Chase has described him as someone who was responsible in everything he did, whether it was at his job or in his personal life. They are all convinced that he would not have been speeding, especially on what was known to be a dangerous road. His former girlfriend says she rode with him on the back of that motorcycle many times, and he was always careful about wearing all his safety gear and obeying the rules of the road, including the speed limit. He was particularly careful with the motorcycle because it actually belonged to a friend of his. He was using it with the friend's permission while the friend was in boot camp.

Their expert, during his deposition, stated that he had relied on a paper addressing the analysis of motorcycle speeds in wreck cases. That article was co-authored by Wade

Bartlett, generally regarded as one of the country's leading experts on motorcycle wrecks. Whenever I pointed out to the attorney for the insurance company how we had two experts versus their one, he basically said that "experts say what they are hired to say." So I was getting nowhere. I woke up in the middle of the night shortly thereafter and decided what I was going to do. Within 24 hours of waking up I had contacted Wade Bartlett and had retained him to review the case. There was too much at stake for Chase not to go full steam ahead. We were going to have three experts!

After we sent Bartlett everything in the file that had been reviewed by the experts, including the police photos, he called me back after he had reviewed everything and confirmed that their expert had misapplied the contents of his article and that our experts' conclusions were accurate. I made arrangements for him to fly to Raleigh and we videotaped him analyzing the wreck, with a model motorcycle and model truck and he demolished the basis of the insurance expert's opinion. We played his 32-minute video at the mediation. And we were able to settle the claim, even after it had been originally denied, for all of the insurance. I knew we were right and I knew that Chase needed every penny we could recover. Kudos to the insurance company and its lawyer for finally accepting responsibility.

I can't think of a better case to illustrate how important it is to have adequate insurance coverage and the right experts.

"When I selected Bob to help my family, it was somewhat a leap of faith. I relied on what I had heard about him and what I had observed from his "Attorneys on Call" show. By the time we concluded the case, I knew I had made the right

decision. He left no rock unturned as he pursued justice for my son. The case is over now but I consider him a friend and more importantly, Chase does too. We are both grateful that he went full steam ahead."

~ Jimmy Cayton, Chase's dad

Chapter 7: Resolving Your Case

AS I'VE SAID elsewhere in this book, I think it's important for us as lawyers to remember that most of the people who come to us have never met with a lawyer before. So in keeping with our theme of "know before you need to," I want to talk about how a case progresses.

Preparing Your Case

We'll start right at the beginning. I believe in preparation, preparation, preparation. One thing that has become crystal clear to me over the years is that the best way to maximize your recovery in a case is to prepare your case, from the beginning as if you are going to trial.

Some cases, such as some simple rear-end collision cases, are not too complicated and don't require a lot of preparation or investigation. But other cases that seem simple may turn out not to be.

Let's look at an apparently simple case and how we might prepare to pursue it. In this example, the responsible driver pulls out from a stop sign at an intersection. Our client is on the main road. Our first step in preparation is to get photographs of both vehicles. That means trying to locate the vehicles so that we can take an extensive number of photographs, inside and out. We'll get on-the-ground photos of the accident scene, as well as aerial photos. Google Earth has made that a whole lot easier than it used to be. We can sometimes get all of these photographs without leaving the office.

I always pay attention to the approach or sightline that each vehicle has. In this example, it may be important to find out from our client's perspective, how far they could see the other car stopped at the stop sign. Did the car pull out from a full stop or did it just roll through the stop sign? We look at factors that might have affected each driver's visibility. We look at the angles where each of the respective drivers first saw the other vehicle and whether there were obstructions to either driver's view. What was the time of the day? Sunshine sometimes improves visibility and sometimes it hampers visibility. Every case needs to be completely investigated.

We can't just assume at first glance the position the insurance company might take in a case like this. They may very well say, "Well, our insured driver admittedly pulled out from the stop sign. But your driver had plenty of opportunity to see him and to at least slow down or to perhaps even avoid the collision." Maybe the accident report shows no skid marks, for example, for our client.

Over the years I've learned a lot from accident reconstruction. It's possible, for example, to brake and not leave visible tire impressions. An expert I used recently gave me information about the time of day affecting the visibility of skid marks. Anti-lock brakes can sometimes hamper being able to see tire impressions.

We have to be prepared to counter whatever the insurance company presents as some type of defense to either deny the claim or to at least minimize the value of the claim.

Because, as I have frequently said, even with a fairly clear-cut claim, where the other driver is clearly at fault, you have to be careful that they don't develop some type of contributory negligence, bogus as it might be. They may not necessarily use that to deny the claim altogether, but they may say that they're only going to pay X amount of dollars. They will challenge you to take a chance on a jury finding contributory negligence, which would result in your client recovering nothing. North Carolina's contributory negligence provision can be and is often really harmful, in an unreasonable way, to injured parties in our state.

We always have to be conscious of possible contributory negligence, even if another driver has pulled out from a stop sign or has run through a red light, or has turned left in front of you (like Chase's case) , not yielding the right of way. Even in such obvious claims, if the claimant has serious injuries, there's a lot at stake on the part of the insurance company. They will look for any opportunity to minimize their responsibility or perhaps even eliminate it. For example, if someone pulls out from a stop sign in front of you and you hit them, but the evidence were to show that you were on your cell phone at the time and were somewhat inattentive, then even though the other driver was definitely at fault, the insurance company can deny your claim based on your contributory negligence.

The legal question that's asked is: Did you in any way contribute to your injuries? It only has to be one percent or a half percent, and the end result in North Carolina is that you get zero. Because that's such a favorable result to the insurance company, the adjusters who are assigned the claims know that law well and they are always looking for it.

I tell clients, "don't guess distances or times." For example, the insurance adjuster may ask a claimant who's hit by their insured running through a stop sign, how far away from the intersection were you when you saw our vehicle? If you're not careful, you can unintentionally create contributory negligence.

For example, when I ask that question, one of the most typical responses I get is, "Well, I really didn't see it until it hit me." Let's say the collision occurred in the middle of the intersection. The driver who ran through the stop sign had made it at least halfway through the intersection. It took time to do that. When they started though the intersection, the claimant was back away from the intersection. They may have had the opportunity to see that the defendant was going to run the stop sign and therefore could have taken some action to avoid the collision. That's a typical example of how a claimant can unintentionally create contributory negligence.

Sometimes, when my client says he did not see the other vehicle until the collision, I ask, "Does that mean that that car was dropped out of the air from a helicopter right in front of you?" Eventually they seem to get my point, which is that you probably did see the car before the actual collision. About 99 percent of the time, you do see it before the wreck. You might say that you don't know, it was just seconds and you didn't have time to do anything. That's a better answer than guessing at 200 or 300 feet or whatever your guess might be.

If there is a claim and I'm hired as your attorney, I'm not going to let you talk to an adjuster outside of my presence, either on the phone or in my office. I'm also going to talk to you about what I anticipate the questions to be, well before any recorded statement, so that you don't unintentionally make a mistake.

That brings up something else that I've got to say. This is true in every case, whether you handle it on your own or hire a lawyer, whether you go to court or don't go to court. There's one absolute rule that I insist on, and that is to tell the truth, even if you think the truth might be harmful to you. In today's world with all the technology and the thoroughness of insurance adjusters, they are going to find out the truth. For example, have you been able to go to work since the wreck? "No, I can't go to work. I can't even carry out the trash." Well, then they have a private detective who's got a picture of you carrying out the trash. The fact that you can do that is not as important as the fact that you lied about it. Anytime an insurance company catches a claimant in a known lie, then it has a drastic effect on the recovery that that claimant is going to receive.

The insurance companies know that juries can tolerate a lot of things. They can tolerate a bellyacher. They can tolerate someone who will exaggerate their injuries a little. They won't tolerate that a lot, but maybe a little. But they will not tolerate a liar. They're just not going to do that. It doesn't mean you that you necessarily get nothing, but it will adversely affect your case.

I tell my clients to make an extra effort to just always tell the truth and not worry about the effect of the truth. If you start worrying about it, then you may have some tendency to try to shape your answer. If you are a claimant, I'll try to help you think of yourself as a witness to this wreck and not a participant. You know an awful lot about the wreck. You know a lot about your medical condition. That way you'll come across as a much more objective observer than you will as an interested claimant. If you have good days when you don't feel any pain, admit that. Don't think that it's going to hurt your claim.

There seems to be a lot of myths out there about things that can hurt a claim. One of those is returning to work. Clients will call and tell me the doctor says they can go back to work, but they're not sure they should because it might hurt their case. Well, the clear answer is, go to work. Try to go to work sooner than what the doctor says. That will always look better in your medical record than a notation saying the patient was advised they could return to work, but they do not think they're ready yet. I encourage my clients to go back to work if the doctor tells them to go back. Even if you get there and find you can't do it, at least you're on record with complying with the doctors' recommendation and attempting to do it, as opposed to just unilaterally deciding that you're not ready to go back to work.

Our case preparation also includes putting our hands on all of the medical expenses and any lost wage information. We'll spend time with the client to find out how bad things were during the healing process. Once we have all of that, and our client has reached their maximum medical improvement, we can then present a settlement package to the insurance company. We don't usually refer to this as a settlement demand package, though it's a common term and one that insurance companies use themselves. They'll ask us when we are going to send them our settlement demand. I think it's a better practice to send the package, including everything that pertains to that claim. Unless it's a significant claim, with perhaps catastrophic injuries, we don't usually submit a demand along with the package. We wait until the insurance company has reviewed the package and has determined what it wants to do as far as its first offer.

In preparing the settlement package, I will have made an in-house, fairly informal evaluation of the case, and I'll keep that in mind. But I prefer to take the initial offer from the insurance company and present that to the claimant, our client. That's when we really try to get on the same page with our client regarding a reasonable value, which is usually a range.

I spend a lot of time with clients explaining that with any claim there is the value of the loss to the client, and then there is the value of the claim, and those two amounts are very seldom the same. The value of the loss to the client is usually much greater than what we could reasonably expect the value of the claim to be. The client may have hurt his legs, and he couldn't go to his grandson's football game, or she couldn't go on a planned European trip. That loss has significant value to the client, but it's not going to have the same value to a jury or to an insurance company. That's just one example. Another is inconvenience, like sleeping on the recliner for six months after a wreck because you can't sleep flat on a bed. I believe that is a huge loss in the quality of life, but it doesn't necessarily carry over, dollar for dollar, and increase the value of the claim.

Other things can affect the value of a claim. Maybe the client, for one reason or another, can't communicate well and can't explain the effect that the injuries had on his or her life. Maybe the client would make a bad witness. Sometimes that plays a role in the value of the claim. Sometimes being undocumented, or being a member of a minority group, may affect the value of the claim, because the value ultimately always comes back to the question: What would a jury award? When the insurance company is making its evaluation it's got all kinds of statistics available, and data on all the claims that the company has handled. Much of that data is based on what juries do.

There are not as many jury trials as there used to be, but even when I'm meeting with a client and we're talking about the reasonableness (or unreasonableness) of the insurance company's offer, we've always got to go back to what we might expect from a jury.

Jury verdicts are very difficult, if not impossible, to predict. You can usually come within a certain range—I always like to use a bell curve on the probable outcome—but you can't know for sure. I might figure a case is worth between $50,000 and $70,000, with a small probability of more or less. But there might be a $120,000 verdict from one jury, and there might be a $30,000 verdict from another jury for the same case. I always point out that you can go try a case Monday, try it for three days, get a verdict from that jury, and then take that very same case and try it the following week with another jury, and you may get an altogether different outcome. You'd hope they would be within a reasonable range of each other, but you just don't know.

That's why the prediction of what a jury will do is very difficult. In spite of that, my approach with my client is that they're entitled to have my opinion about it. In fact, that's in part what they're paying for. They know more about their individual injury, but they have no idea how to transfer that to a dollar value. As experienced lawyers, we're not perfect at it, but we can do a much better job of it than the typical client.

I would say that 90 percent of claims are settled via a negotiated settlement. I would even say that 90 to 95 percent of the claims where there's a lawsuit filed are eventually settled.

Usually when we file a lawsuit it is because we have not been able to settle, but I tell clients when we do file suit that the odds are at least 90 percent the case will settle before we get to an actual jury trial.

We now have mediated settlement conferences in any claim in which there's a lawsuit filed. That never used to be the case. We would always prepare a case for trial; now we prepare for both trial and mediation.

It used to be that any negotiating you did after filing a suit was sporadic, maybe when it got close to the trial date. There was a little bit of reluctance for either side to be the first one to try to act like they wanted to settle it—there was a little gamesmanship to it.

Now we have mandatory mediated settlement conferences, which we didn't have back then. That means that at some point in the process of the lawsuit, all of the decision makers will be gathered in a conference room somewhere, sitting on opposite sides, and they'll each give a summary of their respective claims. Our side will explain the reasons we think the claim has a certain value or a certain value range, and the other side will point out the obstacles that we might face with a jury trial. I always find that to be really helpful sometimes for my clients. I encourage my clients to go to mediation with an open mind and an open ear and listen to what that defense lawyer says, because as well as I might lay out the risk and play devil's advocate for them about what could go wrong, I'm not as good at doing that as a seasoned insurance defense lawyer.

What I do is advocate for injured people. While I recognize the risks and the possible pitfalls, I don't believe in those as strongly as a defense lawyer does, and I'll tell my clients that. I tell them to listen to what the defense lawyer has to say, and then we'll talk it over. After each side has its say so in the opening session, we break out into separate rooms. The mediator goes back and forth between the two rooms, conveying the offers and asking questions. Sometimes they'll come to me and ask what I think the reasonable range of a jury verdict would be if we took the case to trial. The mediator will want me to compare that range to the offer that's on the table. Mediators say that if you're able to settle your claim, you're at least in control of it.

You might not be crazy about the outcome, but it could be better than going through a jury trial. We lawyers might love a trial, but it's very stressful for the client who goes through it. It can be a horrible experience for the claimant. It means sitting in front of 12 strangers sharing some very personal medical information, and you're going to be there to ask for money. You're going to have to tell the jury why you think you're entitled to that money. It's usually just awful. I'm not saying it should be avoided in every case, but it's not a pleasant experience for the client.

If you're able to reach an agreement—let's say you settle your case for $7,000 and you really wanted $14,000 or $15,000—where you had a slight chance of a zero recovery, and you have reached the decision to take that, I think sometimes psychologically that's better for the client.

In some cases, particularly death cases, I think losing is particularly horrible for the client. Suppose a decision says there was contributory negligence. The family is left with the idea that maybe the death of their child was partly their child's fault. Or when they get a verdict that's far less than what they expect, a family receives that as some statement from the community about the value of their loved one's life. I encourage settlement as long as it's within a reasonable range.

We very seldom have bench trials. In a bench trial, a judge decides without a jury. Usually in North Carolina, you ask for a jury trial in your original filing, which is called a complaint. If you don't ask for it in your complaint, the defense will usually ask for a jury when they file their response to your complaint.

Distribution of Funds

Once a case has been decided, either through a settlement or a trial verdict, we deal with the disbursement of the funds—in other words, who gets what.

Let's say you settle the claim for $10,000. There are expenditures that have to be made from that $10,000: the attorney fees, any outstanding medical bills, and any costs associated with the case, such as charges for medical records. Then after all those payments are made, the client receives the net amount. Our clients get a summary sheet showing all the recovered amounts, since they may come from different insurance companies if there's underinsurance or med pay involved. We show the total recovery, we show everything that has been paid out, and we show the net amount. We usually hand-deliver a check for that net amount, and have with the settlement package copies of all the checks we've written out to everybody, as well as the supporting documents—that's what we call a disbursement package.

Subrogation

This is a concept that many clients find difficult to grasp. If they have health insurance, whether it's a private plan or a plan through their employer, or whether they have Medicare or Medicaid or military coverage, and they have a recovery in their claim, they may have to pay back that insurance company or Medicare or Medicaid because they have a subrogation claim to their payments. Sometimes, they'll ask me, and they're just as serious as they can be, "Well, why should I have to pay them back when it's this insurance company and their driver that caused me to incur all these medical bills?"

Sometimes I explain it this way: Suppose you fell out of a tree, and that resulted in all the same injuries and medical bills, but there is no recovery because there's no one at fault. Then you would not have to pay back your health insurance or Medicare or Medicaid. It's only when the injury results in a recovery from somebody else's insurance that you have to pay back the health carrier. That term, having the right to recover those proceeds, is subrogation.

Most big employees have what is called an ERISA (Employment Retirement Income Security Act) plan, and that always has subrogation rights. They are very aggressive about getting their money back if there is a claim. One of the first things they do when they pay any medical bills is send a questionnaire to the insured asking how the injury happened, whether there is a claim, whether they have a lawyer, and requesting the lawyer's contact information. Then I get a letter from the plan putting me on notice. Medicare and Medicaid don't have to send us anything; we are automatically deemed to be on notice. We can figure out pretty early in a case whether there's going to be Medicaid or Medicare involved.

Sometimes those subrogation claims are negotiable, and we will negotiate those on the client's behalf. Usually you can negotiate some with an ERISA plan. You can't negotiate with Medicare. With Medicare you have to pay them everything they're entitled to, and then if you think it's unfair to your client, you can request a hardship reduction, but they'll only consider that after they've been paid in full.

Here's an example. Let's say you're injured pretty badly and you have $100,000 in gross medical bills. Medicare pays all your medical bills, and it costs them $50,000 to do it, so you owe them back $50,000. The responsible party only has minimum insurance of $30,000 per person. You have no underinsurance, so you recover $30,000 and you owe Medicare $50,000. What you're required to do is send them the $30,000 with a letter of hardship about what you have been through with the accident and why Medicare should waive it all. Sometimes they do; I usually find them to be fairly reasonable. Whatever they decide, you've got to take it. There's no place you can go to contest it.

King's Story

Whatever the outcome of a claim, the process is always difficult for a client or family. There is never an award that can adequately compensate for a tragic loss.

This was just a heartbreaking story. King was a 2-year-old boy who was just the apple of his mom's eye and his grandparents' as well, and everybody who ever met him.

He was in his car seat in the back seat of his mom's vehicle. He was in an appropriate child restraint seat. His mom's car had a head-on collision with a farm truck on a Sunday evening. The collision hit at an angle, with the left front of the farm truck striking the front right of our vehicle. I've learned from engineering that means the real force would have been on the opposite side of our vehicle, which was where the baby was. King was in the back left and the impact was on the front right. The impact, as he was strapped in his seat, pulled on him with such strength that he sustained serious internal injuries to his spleen and liver without any external injuries other than the belt marks. He threw up, but his mom thought that he was going to be okay.

The driver of the truck tried to restart his truck. When he couldn't get it started, he took off running. He never even stopped to see if anyone else had been hurt.

At the hospital, King's internal injuries were discovered. He had surgery but the damage was too severe. They couldn't stop the internal bleeding, and he died that night.

We filed a wrongful death suit against the farmer who owned the truck and the truck driver, who was his foreman. We got into litigation, and agreed in this case to have an early mediation.

Mediations don't usually happen until you're further along in the case and you've taken the experts' depositions, but we had a mediated settlement conference. We settled the case for a substantial sum of money despite the fact that this was a small child and his heirs had no economic damages.

In a death case, the damages are the loss to his heirs—what support would his mom have lost over his lifetime? What would be the loss of companionship and advice and protection?—that's what our North Carolina statute provides. With death claims for children, a usual range might be between $300,000 and $600,000. This recovery was quite an accomplishment, and I talked to his mom about that. I wanted to let her know that it was a tribute to King and a recognition of what a huge loss she had sustained by losing her little boy.

There was considerably more insurance available, so this young mother—she was only 23—was faced with a choice of trying to recover more by going forward with the case. As young as she was, she very wisely recognized that the possibility of getting more was not worth the risk she would take of getting less, along with the emotional price she would pay for going through a trial.

In a trial, there may have been people pointing the finger at her, over the loss of her child. Over the years I've learned that people make judgments in situations like this. A lot of people think this wouldn't happen to them and their child because they're more careful. That kind of judgment even carries over to a jury. They might have held our mom somewhat responsible.

King was very much loved by the staff at his daycare and was one of the most popular kids there. His mom is using some of the settlement to buy a memorial plaque for King at the daycare. In his two short years on earth he made such a big impact on everyone who knew him. That was a case and special kid I'll never forget.

Chapter 8: When the Worst Happens ...

THIS IS ALWAYS a difficult subject to talk about, but every personal injury attorney deals with cases where someone has died. I've shared several such cases already in other contexts, but in this chapter I want to talk specifically about wrongful death.

Wrongful death cases are a specific category of personal injury law. In these cases the injury is the worst possible, because it results in a death.

Sooner or later, we all experience the death of a loved one. When that death is sudden and completely unexpected, it is always a monumental event. What I've learned over the years from families is just how monumental it is, in many different ways.

Wrongful Death Cases

From my personal experience with both of my parents I understand that even an anticipated death can be difficult to deal with. When it's completely unexpected, as it always is in a wrongful death case, I have found that it's very difficult to predict the emotion, the anger, and the grief of the survivors, whether they're the parents or the children or the siblings of the deceased. I'm very careful in expressing any opinion to these clients about what is appropriate.

The truth is, I think anything they're going through is appropriate. It may be different for different families, and it's certainly different for individuals, but I treat my wrongful death clients and families very gently. That's the way they should be treated; their grief deserves to be respected.

When it comes to the legal ramifications of a wrongful death, North Carolina is what is called a survivorship state, which means the claim belongs to the heirs or the next of kin. With an estate, you have a personal representative—the Administrator or the Executor—but the recipients of a wrongful death settlement are the heirs who may or may not be the Administrator of the estate.

The heirs are determined by law, according to the estate succession statute, which spells out how people's estates will be divided in the absence of a will. You go to that statute and figure out how any wrongful death proceeds would be distributed. For example, suppose we have a family consisting of a husband and wife with two young children. The husband dies in an accident. In his will, he may very well leave everything to his wife, if she's living. But if his death is ruled to be a wrongful death, then the proceeds of the wrongful death claim—not the estate, but the claim—would be divided according to the statute with one-third to the wife and one-third to each of his two children.

As in other injury cases, we prepare a settlement package that includes economic losses like medical expenses for the deceased, funeral and burial costs, lost income, and loss of support. In our example, for instance, if a supporting father or parent is killed and a minor child has 10 more years before they turn 18, then one of the losses to that child is going to be the loss of economic support for those 10 years.

There are also noneconomic losses. In 1965, North Carolina passed a law, sometimes called the Housewife Law, which for the first time allowed the recovery of noneconomic loss in a wrongful death claim. The statue says that the heirs are entitled to the present monetary value of their loss of companionship, guidance, counsel, et cetera.

Another part of the recovery is the pre-death pain and suffering of the deceased. Even in a case where death is instantaneous, there is the anticipation of death, kind of an emotional fear factor. North Carolina recognizes that.

In these cases, I've found that most families just want answers. They want to know what happened. They want to know what caused the death, and what mistake led to that. They want some type of justice and a sense of recognition of the value of the loss of their loved one. And they want someone to be held legally responsible. They don't always get that in the criminal proceeding, if there is one. In a car wreck, for example, the at-fault party may get charged with a crime of death by vehicle. What we do in our business is pursue a civil claim. The best-known example of this is probably the famous O.J. Simpson case. He was found not guilty in the criminal case, but the families of the deceased recovered a judgment against him in the civil case.

The reason for that is a difference in the burden of proof. All criminal cases require proof beyond a reasonable doubt. In civil cases, the burden of proof is called a preponderance of the evidence. It's got to be more likely than not. I like to call it the greater weight of the evidence and I illustrate using my hands to simulate scales. There doesn't have to be a huge weight difference in the scales. They might tilt just slightly, but if it's more likely than not, then that's your burden of proof. If you have to prove, for example, that the defendant was negligent, then you just need to prove he was more likely negligent than not. You don't have to prove beyond a reasonable doubt that he was negligent. I sometimes think I used it better as a criminal defense lawyer, because sometimes the only defense you had was to ask the jury: "Are you really satisfied beyond a reasonable doubt that they've proven their case?"

Unfortunately, the only thing you can recover in a death claim is money, and usually that's the last thing the heirs will say they're interested in. But then when you start negotiating and the other side is saying you shouldn't have very much, that's when they think they should have more. I don't think it's because they want the money. It's because they want the recognition of their loss. They want affirmation of their loved one's value, and the only thing available is money.

They want acknowledgment of the worthwhileness of their loved one. That's something I talk to families about, and this next story is one of the best examples I've seen.

Remembering Cody Blue

Let me tell you about Cody, nicknamed Cody Blue. Cody grew up in Ayden, North Carolina. He was an outstanding student at Ayden-Grifton High School, and attended NC School of Science and Math his junior and senior years of high school. He was excited to be accepted at North Carolina State University.

His mom worked in nursing, and his dad was a construction supervisor, a commercial construction supervisor. Cody was the apple of their eye. He could do no wrong, and actually did no wrong. He was a straight arrow, responsible kid, who never gave them any problems whatsoever. Didn't drink, didn't smoke, never did any drugs.

Cody went to State, hoping to major in mechanical engineering. He pledged a fraternity. His fraternity brothers loved Cody, even though they thought he was pretty square. They loved him anyway. For example, the usual initiation for the pledges was to drink a quart of beer. But Cody didn't drink, so he had to drink a half a gallon of milk instead.

Cody moved into a duplex apartment house near the State campus with his fraternity brothers. It wasn't an officially recognized fraternity house, but they kind of used it that way. It had a living room and a play room on the main floor and bedrooms upstairs.

There were four fraternity brothers living on each side of the duplex—one in the basement and three in bedrooms on the second floors. Cody's parents went to Raleigh to help Cody move into the house.

Cody started working a part-time job at a printing company. The night he died, he had been working and arrived home at about ten o'clock.

It was October of 2005, during the football season. In fact, Florida State was playing North Carolina State in Raleigh. It was a home game for State. At the time, Florida State had been undefeated in the Atlantic Coast Conference (ACC) for years, but State upset them that night. So there was a lot of partying going on at the apartment.

Cody had to go to work the next morning, so when he got home, he visited very briefly with the guys on the main floor and then went on up to his room and went to bed.

During the night a fire broke out very slowly on the main floor—somebody must have left a lit cigarette or something. The fire spread. It didn't really burn the house down completely, but it caused substantial damage. Cody was killed in his bedroom upstairs. His body was not burned; he died from smoke inhalation and heat.

There was another occupant in a bedroom upstairs adjacent to Cody's. The dad of that kid had noticed that there didn't appear to be any smoke detectors in that apartment. He had put one in his kid's room and it woke him up. He had to jump out of the second floor window. He broke his leg, but he survived. A third roommate on that floor was found dead in the bathroom.

Cody's dad showed up in my office to interview me. He wanted to do something about what had happened. He was burdened with a huge sense of guilt himself for not having noticed the absence of smoke detectors, especially since he was in the construction business. He knew that the smoke detector had made the difference in the roommate's surviving. This whole family was just crushed.

His mom was notified by a local sheriff. He came to see her saying he had something he needed to tell her and it was not going to be easy. He told her that he'd gotten a report from Raleigh and that her son, Cody, had died in a fire in the dormitory. She thought he was mistaken. She told us, "Well, I just said, well no. You got it wrong. That's not Cody. He lives in an apartment." Of course, it turned out to be Cody. The sheriff had just misnamed the place.

Cody's death just devastated that family.

When I started investigating, all I knew was that there had been a fire in an apartment. I had to start from scratch.

The first thing I did after reading the fire report was hire a fire expert, an engineer who specializes in such cases.

I was concerned about a lot of things. I knew we probably couldn't identify and hold responsible the person who left the cigarette lit.

We began investigating, my expert and I, and as we were going through the apartment house, he opened a hall closet and on the shelf found there were about eight unopened smoke detectors. Because the receipts were in the bag, we had the date they had been purchased.

We identified the owner of the apartment, who was a businessman in Raleigh, but more importantly, we identified the management company that he had hired to manage the property. We sued both the owner and the management company.

The management company had hired a college kid who didn't know what he was doing to put in the smoke detectors. He never did, and they never were checked. We took the deposition of the kid who had bought them.

Our theory of the case was not so much to hold them responsible for the fire itself, but to hold the owner and the property management company responsible for the lack of smoke detectors. They tried to argue that it wouldn't have made a difference, but we could show that it had made a difference for the kid who survived.

I learned that the smoke detectors should actually have been in the hallway on that second floor and in each of the respective rooms. The one kid who had the alarm heard it late. He couldn't reach anyone else; he had to jump out the window.

Cody's dad helped me realize what families wanted and needed to know. He wanted to know the details of how Cody died. He told me, "Bob, I don't care how bad it is. I just want to know." I was able to see the photographs of the body and when I told him, he insisted on seeing them.

We worked the heck out of that case. We put a lot of effort into the video we made for the mediation. We included footage of Cody as a kid, and some images from the funeral. I remember his third grade teacher talking and saying she'd just never had a student like Cody. Cody had asked her how much a sperm whale weighed.

The case was a dog fight, though. The property owner blamed the management company. The management company said smoke detectors didn't make any difference. There was some argument about whether the code really required them. We were finally able to resolve the case at mediation.

The family came up with the idea of the Cody Blue Foundation, a nonprofit organization. They created it to spread the word about smoke detector awareness I think that sharing their experience helped his dad to deal with his feelings of guilt, because so many people told him that they had dropped their kids off at school, in worse places than that apartment, and never once thought about smoke detectors.

They had a golf tournament every year, the Cody Blue Golf Tournament. The first one was held on the anniversary of his death and we used footage from it at the end of our mediation video. They used the money from the tournament in their program to promote the public awareness of smoke detectors. They also started a scholarship fund in Cody's name.

Their work on smoke detector awareness helped that family to turn the corner. I'll never forget that case, and I'll never forget the Cody Blue Foundation.

Sometimes I share this story with other families in death cases, to encourage them to try to come up with something that will help them find some meaning out of what has happened.

Ashley's Story

Every family deals with death differently, but I haven't often been as inspired as I was by Ashley's family.

Ashley was just 16 years old when she died in October of 2007. Like Cody, Ashley was a special kid. She was just as cute as she could be and everybody we talked to—her guidance counselor, her teachers, her friends—all talked about how she just lit up a room.

I'll never forget one of the stories that Sylvia, her mom, told me. Ashley was on the track team at school. They'd go to the track meet and Ashley would come in last but she would just be smiling and laughing and Sylvia said her husband, Anthony, would be cheering for her just as if she were winning. Anthony was Ashley's stepdad but he just loved her to death.

Ashley volunteered at the local hospital. She helped the patients and she wanted to go into nursing. She also worked part-time at Lowes Grocery Store there in Oxford. I went there and talked to her employers. She was just this perfect little kid, never any trouble. She was the youth choir director at her church—she had a beautiful voice—and she was very active in the church. In fact, the day that she was killed, it was a Wednesday, and they had driven as a family to the church for the Wednesday prayer meeting, where she sang a solo.

The family lived on a road where the speed limit was 55 mph, and this happened after dark. The stepdad was driving, Sylvia was in the front passenger seat, and Ashley and her stepbrother were in the back seat. They had stopped to make a left hand turn into their driveway of their home and while they were stopped, they got rear-ended pretty violently by a young kid whose father was an insurance agent in town. They got pushed off of the highway, to their right, into shallow woods. There was something about the way he hit the back of the car, that caused Ashley to get hit really hard. Sylvia had to get into the back seat to try to talk her through it. She said her eye didn't look right. I later learned from the medical records that her eye was missing from the impact; it got hit in some kind of strange way. Basically, this poor girl bled out and died holding her mom's hand, right in front of their home.

The family came to me because they had received a letter from a lawyer representing Ashley's biological dad. He wanted them to join him in bringing a wrongful death case. They didn't want anything to do with him, and they wanted to know what their rights were.

The first thing we did was bring a lawsuit against the dad. He was under a support order through their IV–D program to pay a certain amount of child support and he was forever delinquent. He probably paid 60 percent of it over the time period. Based on my years of IV–D experience, I was able to comb through that file pretty knowledgeable about what was going on.

There was a history of domestic incidents from before he and Ashley's mom had separated. He had only had some sporadic overnight visitation with Ashley, and nothing in the last five years. His argument was that he would see her at various times, maybe in the grocery store when she was working, or on the street. He would spend a little time with her then; he would give her gifts occasionally. Maybe three times he gave her a birthday gift; maybe twice in 16 years he gave her a Christmas gift.

Through the old Bob Whitley thorough investigation, we found out that he had been charged with passing some worthless checks. One of them was at Lowes, the grocery store where Ashley worked.

We really dug into that, and interviewed the arresting officer. He had confessed to the officer exactly what he had done, but when we went to trial and I asked him about it, he had concocted some story that it wasn't his check, and he didn't know it wasn't good, and all that. So we put the officer on the stand and just nailed him on that lie. It was a bench trial. We didn't have a jury trial; we had agreed that the judge could make the decision on whether or not he had a right to be an heir. The judge ruled that he had abandoned her and was eliminated as an heir, so Sylvia became the only heir. We were able to resolve the wrongful death case at mediation.

I heard so many wonderful stories about Ashley, but there are two that stand out in my mind. In cases like this, I ask the family to share with me all of the cards and the letters of condolences that they get. It helps me understand better the loss that this family has suffered. One of the letters Ashley's family gave me had come from someone they didn't know. It was addressed to the parents of Ashley, and it went something like this. "You don't know me, but I knew your daughter and I just heard this terrible news about her death. I wanted to let you know that I'm a regular customer at Lowes, where she worked, and I always got in her line. It didn't matter how long it was, because I loved my interaction with her. She made me smile and she made me feel good. The Lord was obviously part of her life, and she shared it. I just thought that you should know what a great job you must have done in raising her." And I'd never found a nugget that powerful.

The other thing that I learned was that the hospital where she volunteered renamed one of the scholarships that they gave to their nursing students after Ashley. In the article announcing it they said they had never before done that for someone who was not a nurse or who didn't work at the hospital.

Those two little stories, to me, told the world everything it needed to know about Ashley. That was all I needed to tell the insurance company at mediation.

That family made such an impression on me. Ashley's friends wanted to do one of those memorial wreaths for her, the kind that sticks in the ground where the accident happened. They had put that out there, over across the street from their house in those woods, right off their driveway. Sylvia told me that she made them take it down. She said, "You know, that young man,"—meaning the kid who had basically killed her, who lived down the road—"he has to drive by there every day, and I know we hate it and nobody hates it as much as we do, but he probably is the next one that hates it the most. And I don't think it's fair to just remind him of that bad mistake he made, every day." The remarkable thing about that family was that they were never angry. Almost all families get angry, though most of them get beyond that. But Ashley's family never even had to move beyond it. And I don't think they suffered as much as some because of that.

Chapter 9: Mythbusting

IN MY YEARS of experience, I have found that some categories of injury cases seem to generate a lot of myths and misperceptions. I think it's important to debunk some of those, so let's take a look at a couple of those areas.

Work-related Injuries

On-the-job injuries make up a specific category of injury cases, the legal term for which is workers' compensation. I think they're worth discussing here because there are so many myths about workers' comp and the people who file claims under worker's comp.

Workers' compensation exists as a compromise between making it easy for a worker to get some compensation and avoiding the exposure to employers for the responsibility in all work-related injuries.

If you are hurt on the job, as long as you're not breaking any safety rules—like not wearing a hard hat or being impaired by either drugs or alcohol—you are automatically entitled to workers' compensation. It doesn't matter how you're injured; it might even be your own fault. You might be running too fast and slip and hurt yourself, or you might get injured because you're not following exactly the best way to do something at work, but as long as you have not deliberately violated a safety rule, it's automatic. This is one way workers' comp claims differ from other personal injury cases, where the injury always has to be the result of somebody else's negligence.

Here in North Carolina, where we have the contributory negligence law I've mentioned elsewhere, a person who's injured has to be free from any fault. That's just not true in workers' compensation arena.

One of the purposes of workers' comp is to provide an easy way for the injured worker to recover. The recovery is limited to wage replacement and the payment of the medical bills associated with the injury. In North Carolina, your wage replacement is based on a formula that pays you a weekly amount that should represent two-thirds of your average weekly wage for the past year or however long you've been working.

In other words, if somebody grosses $300 a week and they're injured so that they're going to be out of work for more than five days, then they would receive two-thirds of that $300 or $200 a week in workers' compensation.

When the formula was first created, I think there was an attempt to make the workers' net recovery equal to their net take-home pay. That's where the two-thirds formula came from. One pitfall of that formula is that employers don't always account for overtime wages in the calculation. Any amount of income that you've received in the last 12 months should be totaled and then divided by 52 to determine your average gross weekly income upon which the two-thirds is based.

The employer computes that figure early in the process. When we know that our client's going to be out any period of time, we go through an audit to make sure that the employer's computation of two-thirds of the average gross weekly income is correct. We often find a slight error, probably as many times as not, and that can make a big difference, particularly when the injured worker's going to be out of work an extended period of time.

The other way that calculation can make a difference is in the entitlement for permanent injuries. If the worker is able to return back to work, but they're left with a permanent injury, then there are various formulas used to determine the lump sum payment they get in addition to their wages for having been permanently injured. For example, in North Carolina, an injury to your spine or back is considered 300 weeks. So if you end up with a 10 percent permanent disability rating on your back, that would be 30 weeks. You, as the injured worker, would receive a lump sum payment of 10 percent of 300 times the average weekly amount, or 30 weeks' worth. If that average weekly amount is off by just even a little, it could really have a significant effect on the total amount of the compensation for a permanent injury.

Do I Need an Attorney for Workers' Comp?

Many workers' comp cases are routine and don't require an attorney; workers' comp pays the injured worker's medical bills and the worker is back at work within two to four weeks. In fact, most of the time, if someone calls us about that kind of an injury, we start by trying to provide them information. We have a DVD entitled *What You Need to Know If You Have a Workers' Comp Injury or a Claim*, so we can offer that and answer questions.

The real issue, and I think when injured workers do need to retain an attorney, is when the injury is serious enough that they're not certain of their being able to return to work. Those kinds of claims can end up being a lot more hotly contested than a routine minor injury.

In the more serious claims, the question is the worker's future entitlement, because technically he would be paid until such time he's able to return to work. North Carolina has recently modified its workers' compensation law. It used to be if you were injured and you could never return to work, you received workers' comp forever, but that's not the case anymore. There are now time limitations on permanent disability.

Sometimes you end up arguing with the workers' comp carrier, the insurance company, over the issue of whether the worker can return to work. Injured workers have to subject themselves to vocational assessment, meeting with a vocational worker who sends them out to interview and find other means of employment. They're not automatically entitled to permanent compensation. They have to be unable to work any kind of a job, not just the job that they were working.

Some workers' comp clients are surprised to learn that there's no recovery for physical pain and mental suffering. The coverage is strictly limited to the medical bills and the loss of income. If there's any future to either one of those, then that's also included.

There are some other requirements that an injured worker has to follow as far as giving written notice to the employer, and filing various forms with the North Carolina Industrial Commission, which is the entity in our state that manages workers' comp claims. Sometimes claimants are surprised and disappointed to learn that the workers' comp carrier—the insurance company and its adjuster—is basically in charge of their medical treatment. They will send you to their doctor, and they will monitor your compliance with that doctor. You do have the right to get a second opinion, but you are going to have to follow the lead of whatever doctor the workers' comp insurance company connects you to.

It's always important for an injured worker to do exactly what the doctor tells them so far as rehab is concerned, so far as keeping appointments is concerned, and even so far as returning to work. Sometimes our clients don't think they can go back to work, but if the doctor orders them to, our advice to those workers is always, "Do what the doctor says. If you get to your job and you simply can't do it, then you need to report that." That is much better than just deciding unilaterally that you're not going to return to work because they could use that against you to terminate your entitlement to workers' comp benefits.

Third-Party Claims

It can happen that you have both a workers' comp claim and a personal injury claim for the same incident. These third-party claims apply when you're injured on the job, but you're injured because of the negligence of a third party. For example, if you're a truck driver and you're in a bad trucking wreck with another driver and that other driver is responsible, then you're going to have your workers' comp claim because you were on the job at the time, but you may also have a third-party claim against the responsible driver. You need to be aware that if workers' comp pays money toward your wages or medical bills and you have a recovery from a third party who was negligent, then workers' comp is entitled to get its money back. It's similar to the subrogation claims we talked about in Chapter 7.

The law doesn't easily permit you to have a workers' comp recovery and get your medical bills paid and then have a third-party claim that also includes the recovery of your medical bills. You just can't double dip. If you have a third-party claim, however, you're not limited the way you are in workers' comp. In the third-party claim, you can recover just as you would in a regular personal injury claim, which would include pain and suffering in addition to the medical bills and the wages.

If you could compare a third-party claim to a stand-alone workers' comp claim for the same injury, the third-party liability claim would usually allow a significantly higher amount of compensation.

I had a memorable case that was an example of a third-party claim. I represented a UPS driver—we'll call him Joe—who was making a delivery of merchandise to a big retail store that sold hardware and fishing gear. He was delivering at night. He parked in the parking lot where he was supposed to park, and as he was walking to wherever he had to go to make his delivery process, he stepped into a hole and fell. The hole was very difficult to see in the dark. Joe sustained a significant ankle fracture, and it seems unbelievable, but it ended up permanently disabling him from being able to do that job, or to do any work where he would need to be standing on his feet. It was just terrible, kind of a freak injury. Of course Joe had a significant workers' comp claim, because he was injured on the job, and we developed a premises liability claim against the company whose property he was on when the injury happened. We had photographs and an expert who was able to render a professional opinion that this was an inherently dangerous place for a hole like that because it was a natural pathway between where he had to park and where he had to go to deliver his tickets or do whatever he had to do.

It's a little like the theory that a department store has a heightened safety requirement in areas where they expect customers to walk frequently. There's kind of a heightened duty to make sure that's safer than maybe the corner of the building where nobody ever walks. For example, in both grocery stores and department stores, there's a heightened requirement that they be safe because the customer's not really looking where they're walking if they're in the aisle looking for merchandise.

We were able to argue successfully and reach a pretty significant settlement with the retailer, which was a third party claim. We did have to deal with the workers' comp lien for UPS.

I do need to point out one thing about third party claims. The third party can't be the employer, or a fellow employee. For example, let's say Joe had been riding as a passenger for some reason and his driver and fellow employee ran off the road and ended up injuring him, maybe even with the same injury. He would not have a third party claim. You can't pursue a regular liability claim against your employer or a fellow employee, though there is a very narrowly defined exception regarding the employer. It would apply if the employer were to do something atrociously deliberate, like shoot you, or push you off a ladder, or something.

A 1991 ruling by the North Carolina Supreme Court in *Woodson v. Rowland* gave rise to what is known as a Woodson claim. A Woodson claim allows an employee to sue an employer for intentional misconduct that endangers employees, but the courts make it very difficult to pursue such a claim.

Injured workers often find that very difficult to accept. Maybe they're working on a piece of equipment that is inherently dangerous and the employer doesn't do everything possible to make it safe. But if they are injured by that equipment, they are still probably going to be limited to a workers' comp claim rather than a liability claim back against the employer. Remember, the whole purpose of the workers' comp law was to eliminate the employer's liability.

Social Security Disability

I want to start out by debunking the biggest myth about Social Security. First of all, Social Security Disability is not welfare. It's essentially a claim for the insurance that a worker has paid into the government throughout his or her work life, through payroll deductions. Some of that money is set aside for Social Security Retirement benefits when you reach a certain age, and some of it is set aside for Social Security Disability (SSD) in the event that you become disabled before you retire.

The people I deal with in North Carolina are really reluctant to file for SSD. It's almost like they're in denial, because to file for it you've got to fill out a form that says you're disabled from any type of gainful employment. That's kind of a tough burden to meet, too, particularly if you're less than 50 years old.

Some statistics indicate that it's significantly more difficult for workers under 50 to successfully pursue a SSD claim than it is for those who are over 50. The test is that the medical condition, injury, or whatever is affecting you, prevents you from any type of gainful employment. That means even being able to be a parking lot attendant, sitting at a booth and collecting money from the people who use the parking lot. That's the minimal type of employment that you sometimes run into when the government's making an argument that you are able to do some work. Your age, educational background, and work experience are all factors in the determination of whether you're totally disabled. For example, take a 50-year-old truck driver who's driven trucks all of his or her work life since the age of 18. If that person becomes disabled from driving a truck, maybe because of a foot injury or an arm or shoulder injury, or perhaps a medical condition like diabetes, it's hard. It's easier to make the argument that the driver really is totally disabled. They just don't have transferable skills. They don't have the educational background to get another job.

That's an easier case to make than someone who is a doctor or a lawyer. Maybe the doctor has hurt his hand and he's a surgeon. He can't operate anymore, but there is probably some other type of employment that he can do. Then it becomes more of an issue of whether that individual is actually disabled. You sometimes get into these arguments over private disability policies. If a doctor has a disability policy, it probably covers him in the very narrow event that he can't go back to practicing medicine. But SSD would be decided on whether or not he could go back to any kind of work.

One question I've been asked a lot lately is whether people on SSD can collect additional Social Security Retirement when they turn 65. The answer is no. You can't collect both, and there is no increase in the SSD payment when you turn

65, or whatever your retirement age might be. The test for SSD is that you've got to be disabled from any type of gainful employment for a period of 12 months. What I've seen is that many claimants come to us late in the process, meaning that their doctor's been telling them for years that they need to file for disability and they haven't wanted to do that. It's just a tough admission for someone to make, particularly if you're only in your 50s, or even your late 40s. I believe it goes back to that work ethic that I have always seen among people in eastern North Carolina and in the people that I grew up with: Everybody prefers to be working.

Do I Need a Lawyer to Apply for SSD?

The process of applying for SSD begins with filling out an application with the Social Security Administration office in your county of residence. The majority of applications—national statistics say about 70 percent, while in North Carolina it's about 75 percent—of the initial applications are denied. If that's the case, you have 60 days to appeal the decision by filing for reconsideration. You can file for your case to be reconsidered and you can submit anything that you didn't submit the first time. Unfortunately, the percentage of denials at that stage is even higher than the initial application. But if your reconsideration appeal is denied, there is a second appeal stage. The second appeal is a request for a hearing before an administrative law judge who will hear your case and make a ruling about whether you're disabled or not. You have 60 days from the date of your reconsideration denial to request a hearing.

At the hearing stage, the rate of approval is much higher; the average in North Carolina is about 55 percent.

If you call us about SSD, we would generally advise you to wait and see what happens with your initial application. We point out that you will probably be denied, and the denial letter will tell you how to file for reconsideration. When you get denied for reconsideration, assuming you do, that's when you need to get a lawyer. The advantage of having a lawyer, at any time, but especially at the hearing stage, is that lawyers will know how to put your medical records together and perhaps even get some doctors' opinions about your disability, and the extent of your disability, that you probably wouldn't have if you were doing it yourself.

We're in the business of organizing medical records, and presenting packages, and making disability arguments every day, in all of our cases. So it's natural for us to be pretty good advocates for people who are disabled, and applying for SSD. In disability claims, the attorney fee is a percentage of your back entitlement, and there is a cap on it. If you are successful in a disability claim, most likely a period of time has passed. Sometimes it's a year; sometimes it's a year and a half or more. But if you're successful and the administrative law judge concludes that you're entitled to your disability, you will get a lump sum for that period of time. Let's say you get $1,500 a month, and it's been 18 months since you applied. You get a lump sum for that 18 months, and then you receive your $1,500 each month going forward. The attorney fee is regulated; it's 25 percent of the lump sum back pay amount, and the maximum is $6,000.

People who are disabled, and have been disabled for a year or two, are the saddest cases, but they're also the most excited claimants of all the people we represent when their claim ends successfully. Usually they've been pretty much broke for a long time. They've worked all their lives, then all of a sudden they don't have any income at all, and then they have to wait a year or two to get the disability income that they were really entitled to all along.

Now in extreme cases there's no question. For example, in Chapter 6 I described Chase's case and the injuries he sustained in his motorcycle accident. He was only 23 at the time of the accident, but his injuries were so acute that his SSD was approved on initial application. There was no question of his being able to return to work.

I'm not saying that everybody has to wait, but the waiting is mainly for those people who are up in age some. They've got a long work history, and they're filing for disability not necessarily because of an acute injury, but maybe because their overall health is bad. It could be high blood pressure, heart problems, diabetes, whatever. You can consider the accumulation of all your medical conditions, and if all of those combined render you disabled, then you're entitled to disability through Social Security.

Chapter 10: Other Personal Injury Cases

THE MAJORITY OF cases that we deal with are accident cases, but there are a few other categories of personal injury cases that we deal with. I want to touch on a few of those in this chapter.

Premises Liability

These are sometimes called "slip and fall" or "trip and fall" cases, because most of these claims involve a client falling or stumbling on somebody else's property. That property may be a department store, a grocery store, or even a residence. Clients sometimes have some trouble understanding that the mere fact that you fell somewhere does not mean that the place where you fell is automatically responsible for whatever happened to you. People fall for all kinds of reasons, but they sometimes forget that.

I find even jurors sometimes think that way. But there has to be negligence on the part of the premises owner for there to be a liability claim. Maybe a grocery store had recently mopped the floor and didn't put warning cones out, or one of the employees had spilled something and was delayed in coming back to clean up the spill. Maybe a customer spilled something from their cart and it was there long enough that it would be reasonable to expect the store to have discovered it and cleaned it up. The law on this is fairly tough.

Another thing that makes premises liability cases difficult is the contributory negligence aspect. Whenever you fall, while you're walking or whatever you're doing, you're taking some action. There's always some room for the insurance side to argue that you weren't being careful enough or you weren't being attentive enough. Remember, even if it's only one percent your fault and 99 percent the fault of the slippery substance on the floor, in North Carolina, you get nothing.

There is a principle in premises liability called <u>diverted attention</u>. There are studies that say that certain products in a grocery store are placed at eye level strictly to draw your attention to them so that you buy them. When you're walking down the aisle in the grocery store, the last place the store wants you to be looking is the floor. They want you looking at their shelves and their products. That means there's a heightened degree of care that they have to give those areas.

Dog bite cases also fall under the category of premises liability, usually covered in an individual's homeowners' policy. We learned in law school the principle that "every dog is entitled to one good bite." The law holds that unless you have some knowledge of your dog's violent propensity, you're not liable. Until you have that knowledge, you're not going to be responsible if he bites someone. Hence, once he gets in his first bite, then you're on notice. That law has been changed some in recent years to consider some breeds of dogs as inherently violent enough to be an exception to that principle. Just owning one of those breeds would put you on notice that they're going to have a tendency to bite or to do something harmful.

One other common issue in premises liability is the idea of an attractive nuisance. An example would be a homeowner who has a swimming pool or a set of monkey bars in their yard. These are things that would be attractive to children.

The Last Mile: Hilda's Story

One of my most memorable premises liability cases happened just a few years ago. My client's name was Hilda; she was a wonderful lady who, unfortunately, is now deceased.

This happened in February of'13. Hilda was 89 years old at the time. She grew up in the mountains of North Carolina and that's where her home place was, she and her husband Henry. They had been married for more than 50 years. They had one daughter who was married and had two grown children; they lived in Raleigh. Hilda's and Henry's health began to deteriorate to where it was difficult for them to live alone without some kind of help. Henry was in the early stages of dementia. Hilda was extremely overweight, diabetic, and legally blind. The way their daughter explained it to me was that they were a pretty good couple in that he could see fine for them to be able to take their medicine, and she had her wits about her—very much so.

So as their health got worse they moved to Raleigh, where they moved into a little apartment. Eventually, Henry died, and the family wanted to take him back to the mountains, where they have a cemetery plot, for his funeral. It's by a little church up on the mountainside. It's beautiful.

The day before the funeral, Hilda's daughter and son-in-law and two grandchildren took her up there to Waynesville, in the mountains west of Asheville, really close to the Tennessee border.

The night before the funeral they went to a local restaurant in Waynesville. It was a small mountain restaurant, very typical of the area. We later learned that this particular restaurant had been in existence for something like 70 or 80 years. About 30 years ago the owners built an addition to it, extending the restaurant to about twice its original size. When they built the addition, or as a result of doing so, it didn't settle completely evenly along the whole plate—along the line connecting the new section and the old. It turned out that the line crossed through the dining room, or at least one of the dining rooms. It ended up being about a two-and-a-half to three-inch difference between the two sections.

And what they did is they put a runner-type carpet over the walkway that concealed the flaw so it was barely visible. It wasn't really visible at all. Now, if you looked carefully at both sides—if you really paid attention and somebody said you're going to have to walk up there and figure out if there's any change in elevation—you might have figured it out. But in normal ordinary use you wouldn't have noticed it. So when the family went to this restaurant, Hilda was in a new transfer chair that they had recently bought for her. A transfer chair is similar to a wheelchair but the wheels are much smaller and it's lighter weight. It's just used basically to push somebody. It doesn't have the big wheels that allow the person to move it by herself.

They parked outside of the restaurant. When they went inside, into the dining room to their table, the grandson was pushing Hilda. On the way to their table, they were going downhill on the change in elevation. There were no warning signs and no one mentioned a need to be careful; nobody did any of that.

After they had their dinner, on the way out, the grandson was again pushing Hilda. But because of her weight, when they came back up on that carpet where the line is, the front wheels of the chair hit it just enough and it was like running into a wall.

But it wasn't a wall. She would have been better off if it had been, because then Hilda wouldn't have been thrown out of the chair. She broke her leg and had to go to the hospital there in Waynesville. She was transported overnight to Duke, in Durham, North Carolina and had to undergo surgery on her leg the next day—the very day of her husband's funeral. The family decided to go ahead and have the funeral; they made arrangements to videotape it for Hilda. Hilda was not able to bring herself to watch the funeral . . . it was too heartbreaking for her.

She was in constant pain from her leg but she was a tough old lady, intelligent and completely alert mentally. What I remember from the times I met with her and talked about it, is that she always came back to the fact that she was not able to attend Henry's funeral. The way she would always put it was, "I was not able to go with him that last mile. And I'll never, ever get over that."

I would ask her, "Well, does your leg hurt?" "Yeah, my leg, it kills me." And she became even more handicapped. But to her, the biggest thing was not being able to go to her husband's funeral. She couldn't stop talking about that. It became the theme of my case: It was the last mile case.

Things like that just don't happen. Think about it: being married that long and then, because of somebody's negligence, you can't attend the funeral. It grew on me gradually; at first it didn't seem as big a deal to me as it really was to her. I always get worried when that happens. When I meet a client, I always try to record my first impression because that's the only impression a jury's going to have. They won't be able to spend as much time on a case as I do, getting to know and understand the client. A jury will get only a day or two or three, and in this case, they would have only a part of that time listening to her talk about the last mile. I was a little concerned at first, but the more I focused on that case and discussed it with people, I found that other people were angrier about it than I had been. They were angry on Hilda's behalf. And so was I!

We sued not only the owners of the restaurant but also the owners of the property. It was hotly contested. During the course of the case, Hilda died, and that's when I went up there to that little hillside gravesite. It was a beautiful setting. All I could think about was that she would have been there about a year and two months earlier burying her husband.

We were able to hold the parties responsible because the law considers a hidden defect like that almost inherently dangerous. The restaurant not only had the defect in the floor, but they did everything they could to conceal it and didn't have any warning signs or any warnings from the staff. The owners of the restaurant took the position that it had been that way for 30 or however many years, and they'd never had anybody get hurt. They argued that they had no reason to believe it was dangerous.

I kept thinking on it, and one day while we were up there taking depositions, I was at the restaurant and noticed that they had these carts that they used for bussing tables. The bus carts had little wheels on them. It dawned on me that the staff would have to deal with that every time they went in and out of there. We started taking the depositions of the wait staff. I got them to talk about the carts. I had one of the carts there and I said, "Now, how did you push that around? Did you just push it around like pushing it forward?" And the girl I was deposing said—I'll never forget it—"Oh yeah, I pushed it everywhere except when you had to come out of that dining room across the crack in the floor. You had to pull it because the wheels would run right into it."

I asked her if anyone had ever gotten hurt there. She said, "Well, there's been a lot of close calls, but everybody knew about it. We called it the crack in the floor. Everybody talked about that crack." That's when the case took a turn for the better.

We had the family's receipt from the restaurant that night and so we had the name of the manager who had seated them. She had left the restaurant and was living in Texas. When we were taking the depositions, they told us they didn't know where she was located, but we found her. While we were taking the owners' deposition, the private detective that we hired in Texas was interviewing that manager, and she was telling him about some incidents with the crack in the floor.

Hilda was just a delightful lady. I'll never forget her, and she was right to speak out about what bothered her. Missing Henry's funeral was a huge loss for her, and it made the last year of her life a whole lot more miserable than it ever should have been. When she died, the insurance company said, "Well, now your client's dead, so that's certainly going to reduce the value of your claim." I argued that while it put a limit of time on her suffering, for her the case never ended. Throughout her own last mile, she had to struggle with that.

They even tried to argue contributory negligence, talking about how visible the crack in the floor was. I pointed out that my client was legally blind and not in control of the wheel. Any negligence would have had to go against her grandson who was pushing the chair. And even insurance companies don't do things that bad, accusing the grandson of contributing to his grandmama's funeral-ending injury.

In the end we were able to secure a pretty good settlement, which went to her daughter as heir. That was certainly one of my most memorable premises liability cases and I will never forget Hilda.

Pharmaceutical Claims

We also handle pharmaceutical claims, when a manufacturer or a company fails to adequately warn the consuming public or the prescribing doctors of the dangers of certain drugs or medications. When a pharmaceutical company has a drug that's making them a lot of money, they're going to be very reluctant to put too many disclaimers in their marketing or on their product that might reduce their sales.

I can think of a few examples over the years. Baycol was one; it was a great treatment for high cholesterol, but it also caused muscle damage and was eventually pulled from the market.

We're currently involved with a claim dealing with a German company that makes GranuFlo, which is the liquid substance that flows through your body when you're on a dialysis machine. There have been reports of side effects and even deaths of dialysis patients, and again, they failed to warn the public.

We were contacted by a big firm in Maryland that handles a lot of that kind of litigation. They wanted to partner with us for these GranuFlo claims. They were targeting eastern North Carolina because of our demographics—a population with a lot of obesity and diabetes, so higher than average numbers of dialysis patients. The criterion for taking a case was that the patient had to have died while receiving the treatment on the dialysis machine, or within 24 hours thereafter.

I couldn't believe we were going to get many cases that met those criteria. We ran a radio campaign for two weeks, and within about four weeks, we had signed up about 300 cases. A lot of the clients that we signed up talked about friends that they used to know at the dialysis center and then they weren't there anymore. I was flabbergasted.

Over time, the parameters for those cases have narrowed and become more limited, but we still have over 100 of those cases. The Maryland firm handling the litigation is trying to work out a settlement with the manufacturer.

As with products like Baycol and Fen-Phen, the profits for these pharmaceuticals companies are just overwhelming. They're worth billions and billions of dollars. The companies almost look at litigation as a cost of doing business. They set aside money, so many hundreds of thousands or millions of dollars, sometimes even hundreds of millions, to pay the people they kill along the way.

I've seen that kind of thinking in other types of businesses. I've handled several railroad cases over the years, and that's kind of the attitude of the railroad companies. In making a decision about a country crossroads and maybe putting up lights and arms that come down and block traffic when a train crosses, they do a cost analysis. They set aside a certain amount of money because they figure it would cost them less to pay claims if somebody gets killed than it would cost to equip the crossroads correctly.

Companies are getting smarter now about some of their products and they are warning the public. You know all those warnings you see in pharmaceutical ads? You can thank plaintiffs' lawyers for those.

Medical Malpractice

When something goes wrong in a medical procedure, clients often want to assume that the doctor or practitioner did something wrong or was negligent in some way. They find it a little hard to accept the fact that something can go wrong in the absence of negligence. One of the terms you hear often in medical malpractice practice is inherent risk. If there are inherent risks to a procedure, it means something can go wrong in the absence of negligence.

For example, if you are having open heart surgery, one of the inherent risks is that your heart may stop beating and you may die on the table. That can happen even if the doctor is doing everything correctly. Sometimes families have a hard time processing that. If their grandma or their parent or even their child dies in the process of some medical procedure, there's a tendency on their part to immediately assume that somebody must have done something wrong.

Having said all that, there are plenty of cases where actual malpractice has occurred, and the patient, or the patient's family in the event of a death, has a case to pursue. There are many different kinds of malpractice claims, some more obvious than others.

When clients think they may have a medical malpractice case, they should consult a lawyer for at least an initial consultation.

Nursing Home Negligence

When I was a young lawyer, I would occasionally get a call about a nursing home claim. I would usually caution them that it might not be worth pursuing because the client was necessarily in bad health already. That would make a claim difficult to prove and minimize any potential recovery.

That has changed in recent years. People are living longer and more of them are going into nursing homes and assisted living situations. We have come to value the quality of life of the elderly as much as we do younger people, and as I like to say, when they need the best of care, they certainly shouldn't get the worst of care.

As nursing home populations increase, there are more risks for negligence and abuse. As with medical malpractice, if you suspect you or a loved one may have a case, don't hesitate to contact a lawyer for consultation.

Our firm has experience in a wide variety of personal injury cases. We also recognize that we may be the only lawyers that our clients know, and they call us first for everything. If a case does come to us that falls outside of our area of practice, we may involve other lawyers but we always stay involved to make sure that our clients get the expertise they need.

Chapter 11: The Whitley Advantage

A FEW YEARS AGO, I was asked to speak at a national meeting of trial lawyers. My topic was the public image of lawyers, and I began my talk by telling this story.

Pumpkin's Story

The client was deceased, and two of her sisters came to see me about a potential wrongful death claim. I'm going to call her Pumpkin; that was the nickname the family had for her. Pumpkin had gone to the emergency room in a county hospital late one afternoon. She had such extreme abdominal pain that she was doubled over and had to be wheel-chaired in by a family member.

The ER did some blood work and one of the things they determined was that she was pregnant. It was very early and she didn't even know that she was pregnant. The emergency room doctor diagnosed her with irritable bowel syndrome, prescribed some pretty powerful pain medicine for her, and told her that she really needed to see an Ob-Gyn as soon as she could. It was early evening by the time she got home. She took the pain medicine as prescribed, but the pain got steadily worse. Pumpkin died around midnight.

She had an embolism, which turned out to have been caused by a tubular pregnancy. The basis of the wrongful death claim was the fact that the standard of care would have required the ER to eliminate a tubular pregnancy once they discovered that she was pregnant, in view of her pain, and they sent her home without doing that. They compounded the error by giving her the pain medicine that probably kept her from coming back to the hospital as soon as she otherwise might have and it might not have been too late.

Pumpkin was only in her mid-20s. She lived with her boyfriend who was presumably the father of the baby. Her parents were deceased; she had no children and no spouse. Under North Carolina law, her heirs and the claimants in her wrongful death claim were her 16 brothers and sisters. That's right, 16.

We filed the lawsuit and a mediation was scheduled.

Pumpkin's sisters mentioned to me that they were going to be having a family reunion. It was unrelated to the lawsuit; it had already been planned for that summer, and all of the family would be there—not only the 16 siblings, and their immediate families, but also cousins and other relatives. It was going to be a big deal. One of the sisters hosted the reunion at her home. It was out in the country and had a huge yard and a big paved driveway. I invited myself and went to the reunion and I brought a videographer with me. It was a wonderful opportunity for me to interview each one of the siblings about their individual relationships with Pumpkin in preparation for the mediation.

It gave me a chance to speak with each one of them and record what they had to say about their deceased sister. Some of them were fact witnesses about Pumpkin's hospital visit the night she died. With most of them I just was interested in learning about their relationship with her: who she was, and what she stood for, and what they missed most about her.

One of the sisters was tearful throughout her interview. When I asked her to tell us about her sister, I said, "We did not know her, so please tell us about her." She would just bawl, and say, "She was just Pumpkin. That's all I can say. She was just Pumpkin." She couldn't stop crying. It was an emotional day for everybody. It's hard for a family to do that.

We interviewed everyone. I remember there being kids scattered all around the back yard and on the swing set. As my videographer and I were getting ready to leave, I was standing with the sisters in the driveway, and on impulse I said, "You know, this has been so helpful to me, and it's really been moving. I just think it's appropriate that we join hands here in the driveway and let me close with a very brief prayer."

I'm not really a public prayer, but it felt like the right thing to do at the time. I'll never forget their reaction. One of the brothers just yelled out, "Junior! Junior! You got to come here! The lawyer is gonna pray! The lawyer is gonna pray!" Then everybody started yelling to gather the family members together, "The lawyer is gonna pray!"

I left there that day very emotional and feeling like I really knew who Pumpkin was. The humor part of the event did not hit me until later. It was like this was a once-in-a lifetime event . . . a lawyer was going to pray.

When I told this story to my colleagues at that national meeting, I told them we have to do something about our image. It should not be a once-in-a-lifetime event for us to pray publicly, or to show that compassion for our clients and families. (And by the way, we were able to settle Pumpkin's case. I played that video of the reunion at the mediation.)

Why do I tell that story? I absolutely believe that all of our clients deserve better than what the public image of lawyers would lead them to expect. I also believe that clients who come to our firm do receive what we like to call the Whitley Advantage. It's a combination of things, and it's always been my concentration in my practice.

It's not only what I learned as a kid growing up here in North Carolina. It's not only the things that my dad taught me, although he did teach me to treat people decently and be nice to everybody, not just those who are nice to you. I recognized early on that clients who hire lawyers are usually involved in something that is not a pleasant experience for them, whether they're hiring a criminal defense lawyer, a divorce lawyer, or a tax lawyer.

The same thing is very true in our practice of personal injury law. Our clients, and probably their families, are going through something really bad or painful. We're about to represent some folks in Raleigh who have been displaced from their condominiums by a bad fire in an adjacent building. They're going to be displaced for a whole year. Can you imagine getting up one day and then by the next day you don't have anywhere to live and you're going to have to find somewhere to stay and get by for a year? Or think about Chase. One day, he was a healthy young man, with a good job as a restaurant manager, and planning to marry his girlfriend. The next day he's in intensive care with a significant brain injury, beginning months of hospitalization, probably never able to go back to work or live on his own again.

Those are some extreme examples, but it's always a bad situation. I also think that the public image of lawyers is such that people don't come to us with much expectation of being treated courteously and respectfully.

I believe that a part of the Whitley Advantage is our recognition that that our clients are going through a bad time. It's a time that they need the best of treatment, courtesy, and respect, and gentleness, and not the very worst. We pride ourselves on the way we treat our clients and the way we interact with them. We suffer along with them in the ups and downs of their situation. We want them to come away with the knowledge that we care about them as people, and we're going to do the very best we can for them. If we don't do it as well as we would like, or the outcome is not what we or the client would have hoped, we suffer with that too.

A large part of world class service is being accessible. Part of the Whitley Advantage is we do not screen phone calls. If you call and say I would like to speak to Bob Whitley, you're going to be transferred to me. Nobody's going to say, "Who may I say is calling?"

It's also returning phone calls, and having a willingness to meet with clients whenever they need to talk to a lawyer about their case. It means going the extra mile, finding the right expert who's going to work best in their case.

The human element of what we do is always the most important, but in speaking of the Whitley Advantage, it's also important to talk about the tools we have now that we didn't have when I first started. The way we work has evolved over the years; we've added—and keep adding—new tools as they become available so that we can stay current.

For example, now I can sit in my small conference room in Raleigh, with a big screen TV on the wall, and talk with a client who's sitting in a conference room in Kinston with a big screen TV up there. That's one way things have changed.

Back when I was doing that IV–D work in Kinston, the child support enforcement, we had so many orders of contempt, and it was all just repetitive typing. We didn't have word processing then. I kept trying to figure out a better way we could do these child support orders because they were all so repetitive, like filling in the blanks. I somehow found a brand new IBM memory typewriter. It was a brand new product, and it was about the size of half my desk. It was huge. It was similar to a Selectric typewriter—if anyone remembers those—but it was much bigger. It had a big dial on the right side, with 50 little numbered notches on it. You could type up to about a page of text, hit a button, and save what you had typed. You could save up to 50 pages. When you came back to print the same document again, you could turn to that same number, hit print and it would print.

It sounds quaint now, but in the '70s that was such an advanced product that other lawyers in town came by to look at it. You could even include some variables, like a place on the page where it would stop and you could type in the name of the person. Then it would keep going.

I used to get phone messages on pink slips on a spindle on my desk. Now, of course, we get emails and voicemails with phone messages and we all have cell phones that make us much more reachable.

All the technology has changed. Now we can sit in court rooms and pull up cases so easily. We can pull up our exhibits. My son Ben knows a lot more about what's out there and how our practice has changed; he's our technology expert.

We have software that helps us to manage our cases. Back in the '70s or '80s, if a client called me and wanted to know if we'd heard from the insurance adjuster, I had to go pull a paper file to see what notes were in there. Now, with a few keystrokes, I can say, "We followed up with him yesterday and he said it would probably be the first of next week. I'm sorry we didn't call you and tell you that, but I'm glad you called so we can tell you that." It's so much easier to keep up to date with every client.

The tools we have today certainly make things easier in many ways, but in the end it's always about the people.

We are a family law firm. My dad was not a lawyer, but he went to every one of my trials when he could after he retired. He became my unpaid jury consultant. He only saw one case that he thought I should lose, and that was an obscenity case.

With my two boys, I never really expected them to follow me into this work. When they were young, they were never lawyers-in-training. One of them was into science and computers and the other one was a jock who played baseball and all the sports. It was only later in their lives that they started expressing any interest in law.

It surprised me some, particularly my younger son. My older son, Whit, well, we had him when we were babies ourselves. He's 20 years younger than I am part of the year, and 19 years younger the rest of the year. When he was little, I was in undergraduate school and law school and I was working all those part-time jobs, but when you're in school, you're still at home more than you are when you're working.

My younger son, Ben, really got to witness all the crazy hours I worked. On a typical day I'd go home about 5:30 or 6:00, eat dinner and then go back to the office for at least a couple hours every day. We didn't have the technology then to be able to work from home like we do now.

It's a thrill having them with me and watching them do this. I'll walk down the hall sometimes and I'll hear Ben arguing with an adjuster. He sounds a little loud, and a little hot-headed, and I'll remind myself, that was me 30 years ago.

In a way, I've come full circle. About five years ago we experimented with running our *Attorneys on Call* show on Sunday mornings in Winston-Salem on the local NBC station. Almost immediately we began to get a lot of calls and some pretty big cases, so after a year or so we concluded that we needed to have an office in Winston-Salem.

Remember that tax law job I took in Winston-Salem when I was just out of law school? The one in the Wachovia Bank building, the finest building in town? Working in that building was like working in a palace.

Well, that was 40 years ago, and that building is no longer the Wachovia Building. Now it's called the Winston Tower, and on the 25th floor you can find the Winston-Salem office of the Whitley Law Firm. The first time I went up there to meet a client, it was like Nostalgia Avenue.

But when I entered the lobby, I found it's not the elegant place I remembered. It's barely a lobby, and it's certainly not marble and wood. The elevators all look like freight elevators and everything is 40 years older. It didn't really hit me until I went into the men's room and saw the old spoked spigots that you turn, one for the hot water and one for the cold water. As I was washing my hands, I thought to myself, "This is unbelievable. This building has gotten old just like me." It was just amazing. I guess the closest thing I can think of is going back to your class reunion after 20 years expecting to see the homecoming queen and discovering she's a queen no more.

Maybe none of us compare physically to the way we were 40 years ago, but in every other way these 40 years have been a rich and blessed time.

If I have carried over anything from those early work years to my profession as a trial lawyer, it is the habit of working hard. I feel you must do everything you can to get the best outcome for your client. I can lose a case and be somewhat (I hate losing!) comfortable if I know that I did everything I possibly could to win that case for my client. But if I don't feel like I've done everything, that's a sick feeling. Fortunately I haven't had that feeling very often, but in the rare times I have experienced that, it's always been kind of a wake-up call. It's a motivation for me to always do the best I can. I eat, drink, and sleep thinking about whatever case I'm working on. And I can do that now much better than I could back in the early years. As a young lawyer I had so many different kinds of cases, but none were so big that I could drop everything else I was doing to work on that. These days I do have that privilege.

The cases and the stories that I've shared in this book, some of them I think about all the time. All of these people and families were wonderful people. I think of Hilda, not being able to go the last mile with her husband. I can't forget Alicia, and her mom's determination to prove she wasn't responsible for her own death. I won't forget little Ashley up in Oxford who worked at the grocery store and at the hospital.

It's been just one after another. They haven't all been perfect, but they have all added something to my life. I think they've made my life better. There's no doubt about that. I hope they have benefited from having the Whitley Advantage. I know it has been our advantage in having represented these people.

And not only have I had this wonderful experience with so many different people who've made an impression on my life, I've also gotten to dig in and learn things I would have never learned if I had stuck to my original goal of being a tax lawyer. I've learned about trains. I've learned about swimming pools. I've learned about tractor-trailers. I've even learned about construction.

I'm very blessed to have been exposed to such a wide range of individuals and families and problems and situations that I could help them with, to whatever extent I have been able to do so. I can't imagine anything that's more pleasurable than what I do.

In Conclusion

FIRST OF ALL, I want to thank you for taking the time to read this book. I hope I haven't bored you with stories that mean so much to me. I also hope that you might think about some of the things I've said and some of the people that you've met through my stories—and remember them the next time you see someone in a cervical collar sitting in your doctor's waiting room, or when you hear about a lawsuit being filed.

I have never brought a lawsuit on behalf of a client who really wanted to file a lawsuit. I've never had a client tell me, after a lawsuit was over, no matter how it turned out, that it was a great experience. It's not. I've found that many clients, when we go to court, are almost flabbergasted at how the insurance company or the defendant tries to make them seem dishonest. They question every doctor's visit and every note that's in a medical record that says they felt better that one day. I think it's always surprising to our clients once we get into litigation—if we ever do in their case—how adversarial it is and how hotly contested everything is.

As I said earlier in this book, I have always found that honesty truly is the best policy. The best thing to do throughout your medical treatment, throughout your interviews with an insurance adjuster, or even in a deposition or trial is to absolutely tell the truth. Do not be afraid of facts that may appear to be harmful to you, like how quickly you were able to return to work. It's hard to refrain from being defensive, but I always counsel clients to just answer questions and furnish information like an uninvolved witness. It's not up to the client to defend their position or even defend their claim; that's what we lawyers do. We are the advocates and our clients serve to provide the facts.

We in North Carolina have a very conservative state with conservative jurors. We don't have runaway verdicts. I also want to be on record stating, as lawyers who do what I do, that we hate frivolous lawsuits, and much less would we ever bring one. When we sign our name on a complaint that starts a lawsuit, we are acknowledging that we are in good faith in bringing the claim. If any client or potential client of mine wanted to pursue something that was the least bit fraudulent or invalid or frivolous, we just simply wouldn't participate in that.

So when you see that person in the doctor's waiting room, and they're wearing a cervical collar, and you might once have thought that they were trying to take advantage of the system, I would like you to remember that they don't want to be wearing that collar and they don't like being in a doctor's office.

I have had a very blessed career. I have met a lot of different people from across my state. I've really never had a client I didn't like. I just think that all people, myself included, have a few little quirks or flaws. Some of my clients have had them, but I have just found them to be very honest people.

They're people who only want to get their life back; people who do not want any more than what they're entitled to. It has been my honor and blessing to have represented them in the best way I know how.

About the Author

Bob Whitley has North Carolina in his blood. Ultimately that's why he came to represent the hard-working folks he labored with in tobacco fields and saw along his paper route. "I just wanted to be a lawyer, and I have an affinity for eastern North Carolina," says Bob, who started his career in criminal and domestic law. "I learned that I wanted to be more involved with people, so personal injury was natural." After 40 years in PI, with a concentration in catastrophic injury and wrongful death, Bob knows that everyone deals differently with trauma. "An unexpected death is one of the most emotional, riveting experiences a family can have, especially when it's the result of someone else's poor decision," he says. "I appreciate the uniqueness of every client. Everyone reacts differently, and there's no right or wrong reaction." This special understanding is often why clients choose to work with Whitley Law Firm. "Being a family firm, we have those family-type relationships. It doesn't mean you become the best friend of every client, but you have to be sensitive and respectful to each client. "There are a million lawyers who know the law, but our advantage is the service we give. We want clients to know we tried as hard as we could and treated them respectfully. When it's all over, we want them to be glad they chose us, and to not just be a fan, but a raving fan, of the firm." Nothing in this profession is better than a satisfied client.

www.ExpertPress.net